G000131029

# *How to Develop Your*
# PERSONAL MANAGEMENT SKILLS

# How to Develop Your PERSONAL MANAGEMENT SKILLS

JANE ALLAN

Copyright © Jane Allan 1989

All rights reserved. No reproduction, copy or transmission of this publication may be made without written permission.

No paragraph of this publication may be reproduced, copied or transmitted save with written permission or in accordance with the provisions of the Copyright Act 1956 (as amended), or under the terms of any licence permitting limited copying issued by the Copyright Licensing Agency, 7 Ridgmount Street, London WC1E 7AE.

Any person who does any unauthorised act in relation to this publication may be liable to criminal prosecution and civil claims for damages.

First published in Great Britain in 1989 by
Kogan Page Limited, 120 Pentonville Road,
London N1 9JN

Reprinted 1990

**British Library Cataloguing in Publication Data**

Allan, Jane.
How to develop your personal management skills.
1. Management skills. Development
I. Title
658.4′07124

ISBN 1-85091-651-9
ISBN 1-85091-652-7 Pbk

Printed and bound in Great Britain by
Biddles Ltd, Guildford and King's Lynn

# Contents

# Preface

This book has been written for anyone who has made management mistakes simply because there was no quick way to find a solution to a demanding problem. Often the answers are there, but they take time to find and sometimes you just don't have the time. This book is intended to make very easy reading and will take you to the solution to your problem as quickly as you'll let it.

There are two ways of using this book:

1. If you recognise any one of the following skills or weaknesses, all you have to do is to turn to the relevant chapter and read. The chapters include examples of forms and checklists wherever possible to make the use of the information easier.

   - Chapter 3, Personality
   - Chapter 4, Staying Calm
   - Chapter 5, Dealing with Change
   - Chapter 6, Creative Thinking
   - Chapter 7, Decision Making
   - Chapter 8, Leadership
   - Chapter 9, Meetings
   - Chapter 10, Assertiveness
   - Chapter 11, Time Management
   - Chapter 12, Making a Presentation

2. If you know you have a problem, but don't know how best to categorise it, you will want to turn to Chapter 2 before reading any further. Chapter 2 is made up of the kind of questions, rhetorical or open, that you may ask from time to time during your business life; questions that need answers, which take time to find. Chapter 2 tries to direct your mind to some of the solutions that lie within the other chapters of the book. Not all of the chapters suggested will be the obvious place to look, but they may well offer the right solution, however surprising.

Finally, Chapter 1 should be reread from time to time. It bears the title *Who Am I?* An answer to that question, given in total confidence, will help you to improve as a manager and as a person. Knowing yourself, and liking what you know, is half the battle to becoming a practitioner of excellence. If you use this book as a helpmate, there on the shelf to offer you a tried solution to the problems you encounter, it will stand you in good stead for many years. You will wish to turn to Chapter 1 at fairly regular intervals, however, because as you change and grow, you will need to re-establish that self-understanding as a base for the next level of growth.

*Jane Allan*

# *Chapter 1*
# Who Am I?

## Introduction

When you wish to achieve something in business, you go to a great deal of trouble to research the background and find all the known facts. That is simply part of putting a good case together and no manager would think twice about doing so. Indeed, if you don't do sufficient research, achievement of the objective becomes far harder, because lack of knowledge means that you give an advantage to any opponent.

The same depth of understanding is required if you wish to improve your personal management skills, and the same pitfalls await the ignorant. Finding out about yourself is hard: it means facing up to the whole truth rather than the truth as you might prefer to see it. Learning who you are might mean knowing about someone who has some unlikeable characteristics. There might be traits in your personality that you are ashamed of or embarrassed by; but, rest assured, if you choose to ignore them, others will still spot them just the same and attack you on your weakest flank. Knowledge leads to understanding, and understanding can teach you tolerance, growth and how to change.

This book will deal with some of the major problem areas experienced by everyone at times. To use it effectively, you need to use the checklists and forms to ensure full self-understanding. Once you know the truth – both the good and the bad – turn to the decision charts in Chapter 2 and follow through to the sections of the book dealing with your area(s) of weakness. Most people find more than one area of weakness: some then make the mistake of trying to change everything at once. Don't be over-ambitious; make a list of the improvements you wish to adopt and introduce them gradually over a reasonable period of time. That way your changes will be more comfortable for all to live with and, what's more, they'll last.

## Which words best describe you?

To determine what type of person you are, and hence your weaknesses and strengths, read through the following checklist and decide which words accurately describe your personality. As you read across the page, you will find that the words describe more intense degrees of a similar feeling. If you feel that the bulk of words in one type applies to you, you can judge your degree of approach from the individual columns most frequently ticked. Of course very few people conform to one type alone. The most dominant section will indicate how you are likely to react, however.

*Type 1*

| 1a | | 1b | | 1c | |
|---|---|---|---|---|---|
| Confident | ☐ | Bold | ☐ | Arrogant | ☐ |
| Independent | ☐ | Individualistic | ☐ | Belligerent | ☐ |
| Competitive | ☐ | Self-centred | ☐ | Ruthless | ☐ |
| Critical | ☐ | Adventurous | ☐ | Domineering | ☐ |
| Self-starter | ☐ | Authoritative | ☐ | Highly individualistic | ☐ |

*Type 2*

| 2a | | 2b | | 2c | |
|---|---|---|---|---|---|
| Outgoing | ☐ | Gregarious | ☐ | Superficial | ☐ |
| Sociable | ☐ | Fluent | ☐ | Garrulous | ☐ |
| Friendly | ☐ | Stimulating | ☐ | Glib | ☐ |
| Talkative | ☐ | Enthusiastic | ☐ | Insincere | ☐ |
| Cheerful | ☐ | Good mixer | ☐ | Highly persuasive | ☐ |
| Optimistic | ☐ | Articulate | ☐ | Loquacious | ☐ |

*Type 3*

| 3a | | 3b | | 3c | |
|---|---|---|---|---|---|
| Relaxed | ☐ | Passive | ☐ | Phlegmatic | ☐ |
| Patient | ☐ | Slow | ☐ | Unresponsive | ☐ |
| Stable | ☐ | Easy going | ☐ | Lethargic | ☐ |
| Methodical | ☐ | Unhurried | ☐ | Very slow | ☐ |
| Calm | ☐ | Well co-ordinated | ☐ | Laissez-faire | ☐ |
| Amiable | ☐ | Deliberate | ☐ | Stolid | ☐ |
| Slow learner | ☐ | Laid back | ☐ | Apathetic | ☐ |

*Type 4*

| 4a | | 4b | | 4c | |
|---|---|---|---|---|---|
| Accurate | ☐ | Precise | ☐ | Perfectionist | ☐ |
| Careful | ☐ | Cautious | ☐ | Avoidant | ☐ |
| Loyal | ☐ | Devoted | ☐ | Servile | ☐ |
| Thorough | ☐ | By the book | ☐ | Dependent | ☐ |
| Neat | ☐ | Fussy | ☐ | Guilt feelings | ☐ |
| Conservative | ☐ | Worrier | ☐ | Yes-man | ☐ |
| Self-disciplined | ☐ | Defensive | ☐ | Aggressive | ☐ |

*Type 5*

| 5a | | 5b | | 5c | |
|---|---|---|---|---|---|
| Unassuming | ☐ | Timid | ☐ | Fearful | ☐ |
| Unselfish | ☐ | Submissive | ☐ | Docile | ☐ |
| Agreeable | ☐ | Easily discouraged | ☐ | Meek | ☐ |
| Peaceful | ☐ | Unobtrusive | ☐ | Self-effacing | ☐ |
| Amenable | ☐ | Self-depreciating | ☐ | Frustrated | ☐ |

*Type 6*

| 6a | | 6b | | 6c | |
|---|---|---|---|---|---|
| Reserved | ☐ | Retiring | ☐ | Private | ☐ |
| Quiet | ☐ | Shy | ☐ | Distant | ☐ |
| Serious | ☐ | Self-conscious | ☐ | Secret | ☐ |
| Sincere | ☐ | Taciturn | ☐ | Remote | ☐ |
| Introspective | ☐ | Imaginative | ☐ | Unsociable | ☐ |
| Pessimistic | ☐ | Day-dreamer | ☐ | Withdrawn | ☐ |

*Type 7*

| 7a | | 7b | | 7c | |
|---|---|---|---|---|---|
| Tense | ☐ | Highly strung | ☐ | Neurotic | ☐ |
| Impatient | ☐ | Driving | ☐ | Explosive | ☐ |
| Quick | ☐ | Intense | ☐ | Volatile | ☐ |
| Restless | ☐ | Very impatient | ☐ | Erratic | ☐ |
| Quick learner | ☐ | Fast pace | ☐ | Impetuous | ☐ |

*Type 8*

| 8a | | 8b | | 8c | |
|---|---|---|---|---|---|
| Bloody-minded | ☐ | Non-conformist | ☐ | Fighter | ☐ |
| Independent | ☐ | Free-wheeling | ☐ | Rebellious | ☐ |
| Stubborn | ☐ | Resistant | ☐ | Undisciplined | ☐ |
| Informal | ☐ | Irreverent | ☐ | Hostile | ☐ |
| Uninhibited | ☐ | Argumentative | ☐ | Insolent | ☐ |

When you have decided what type(s) best describes you, consult the following descriptions of each type to see which chapters you should read to help you improve your management skills.

**Type 1**

- Leaders, people who like to take charge, individualists, entrepreneurs.
- You can be aggressive, bossy, unpleasant, unpopular, tyrannical.
- You probably lack people skills and patience.
- The chapters on staying calm (4) and leadership (8) will help.

**Type 2**

- Pleasant, popular, friendly social types who like people, good communicators and sales people.
- You can be gossips, over-protective, noisy, too hale and hearty.
- You may find management difficult when times get hard and discipline is required. You are unlikely to be an innovator.
- The chapters on personality control (3) and creative thinking (6) will help.

**Type 3**

- Patient, secure, relaxed, an easy-going amiable person.
- You can be lazy, unwilling to change, slow to pick up new ideas, no sense of urgency.
- You will not often try to block change and will find new people and events difficult to adjust to. You lack any sense of urgency.
- The chapters on dealing with change (5) and time management (11) will help.

**Type 4**

- Accurate, organised, efficient, perfectionist. Self-disciplined, conformist, very conscientious.
- You worry about the thoughts of others and often seem defensive. An exacting boss or disciplinarian. Others may find you uncomfortable company.
- You probably find it difficult to delegate and to manage your time.
- The chapters on decision making (7) and time management

(11) will help.

- You should also read the companion volume, *How to Solve Your People Problems.*

**Type 5**

- Unselfish, willing to do things for others, kind.
- You may become discouraged in the face of adversity and lack self-confidence.
- You probably find leadership hard and tend not to get your own way.
- The chapters on leadership (8) and running meetings (9) will help.

**Type 6**

- Strong, silent, analytical thinker.
- You seem to withdraw from others, shy, moody, unsociable.
- You are unlikely to be good at any of the people skills. Don't try to change everything, decide on the important skills and acquire them gradually.
- The chapters on leadership (8) and assertiveness (10) will help.

**Type 7**

- Quick thinker, assertive, doer, person of action.
- People may see you as impatient, intolerant, tense and aggressive.
- You find it almost impossible to stay calm and probably handle time badly.
- The chapters on staying calm (4) and time management (11) will help.

**Type 8**

- Creative, effective delegator, an ideas person.
- People may see you as sloppy, over-casual, stubborn and consider your work to be unreliable.
- You are probably a poor decision maker and poor at running a meeting.
- The chapters on decision making (7) and running meetings (9) are for you.

## What needs do you experience?

Individuals can be classified according to the strengths of their various needs; or, in technical jargon, in terms of a 'recurrent concern for a goal state'. Each need is believed to have two components:

(1) A qualitative or directional component, which includes the object towards which the need is directed.
(2) A quantitative or energetic component, which consists of the strength or intensity of the need towards the object.

Henry Murray, an American management scientist, saw the 13 needs he identified as learned, rather than inherited, and activated by cues from the environment. Thus, an individual might have a need but only pursue the need when the environmental conditions were appropriate, and so the need becomes *manifest.* These needs are as follows:

- *Achievement:* The aspiration to accomplish difficult tasks and to maintain high standards. A willingness to work towards distant goals and to put forward effort to obtain excellence. Any individual experiencing this need responds positively to competition.
- *Affiliation:* An enjoyment of being with friends and people in general coupled with a willingness to make friends easily and to make the effort to do so.
- *Aggression:* An enjoyment of combat and argument. Such an individual may be willing to hurt people who get in the way and seek to get even with people he considers to have done him harm.
- *Autonomy:* A desire for freedom from constraints or restrictions of any kind. Such an individual may be rebellious when faced with restraints.
- *Endurance:* A tenacity and perseverance even in the face of very great difficulties. This individual will not give up easily. Someone who has great patience.
- *Exhibition:* A desire to be the centre of attraction. An individual who seeks an audience.
- *Harm avoidance:* Fear of bodily harm coupled with the avoidance of exciting activities.
- *Impulsiveness:* A tendency to act on the spur of the moment without great thought. This individual may be volatile in

emotional expression.

- *Caring:* A sympathetic comforter who is concerned for others.
- *Order:* A dislike of clutter and confusion coupled with a genuine desire for order.
- *Power:* A desire for control and influence. A spontaneous leader.
- *Succourance:* A seeker of sympathy, love and advice. An insecure individual who readily confides in others.
- *Understanding:* A seeker of knowledge, capable of logical thought.

Perhaps you feel certain needs all of the time; maybe the office brings out the worst in you. Once you know the kind of person you are, assess your strengths and weaknesses, with total and brutal honesty. Don't be falsely modest – there's no one else listening to be impressed by such modesty; don't fool yourself, you'll be the only one.

Take a sheet of paper and on one side write a large plus sign. On the other side, write a large minus sign. You are now ready to list all the positive and negative aspects of yourself and your personal management skills. This list will be your working plan; from it, you will decide what to do and how far to change.

Once you have written your list, put it away and forget about it for a day. After 24 hours have passed take another sheet of paper and prepare a second list of positive and negative points. Compare the two lists: if they are identical, you're ready to take steps: if they don't match, consider the areas of difference and ensure that honesty has applied.

Next, you need to prioritise your list. What are you going to change and what are you going to live with? If you choose to continue to live with certain of the negative points, make sure that you learn to under-emphasise them. Enhance instead the positive aspects of your abilities and character.

Finally, before you turn to the decision charts given in Chapter 2, here's how to change.

## Changing

Sometimes the wanting really is a desire to change. If you think you need to change, you need to work at it. The requirements for change are as follows:

- *Wanting:* To do something, you need to want to do it. Wanting with all of you, not just superficially, is essential.
- *Positives:* Positives work; negatives don't. You need positive motivation.
- *Reward:* Have a reward in sight. To change there must be something in it for you.
- *Power of habit:* Habits are the way the body saves energy. Much of what you do is habit. To deny habit, you need to build new mind channels that override the old ones.
- *Energy builds new pathways, energy comes from contact with people:* Let others help you change.
- *Build a new internal model:* In childhood, you built a model. Now you need to build a new one. Who are your heroes and heroines? In whom do they believe? What is their source of strength? Who makes you feel alive? Who gives you hope?
- *Change produces loss as well as gain:* Everything costs. Consider the price. Are you prepared to pay it?
- *Change a little at a time:*
    - *Record your gains:* Keep records to see progress and achievement.
    - *Have options:* Not everything you set out to do works. Write contingency plans. Know when to stop.
    - *Get help:* Most people need all the help they can get; don't be ashamed to ask for it. Getting help is only effective when you are willing. Stop looking for magic and participate fully in solving your own problems. Help the helper.

*Chapter 2*

# Now What?

## Decision chart 1

**Whenever you hit the busy period of the year, your staff throw tantrums and things don't get done.**

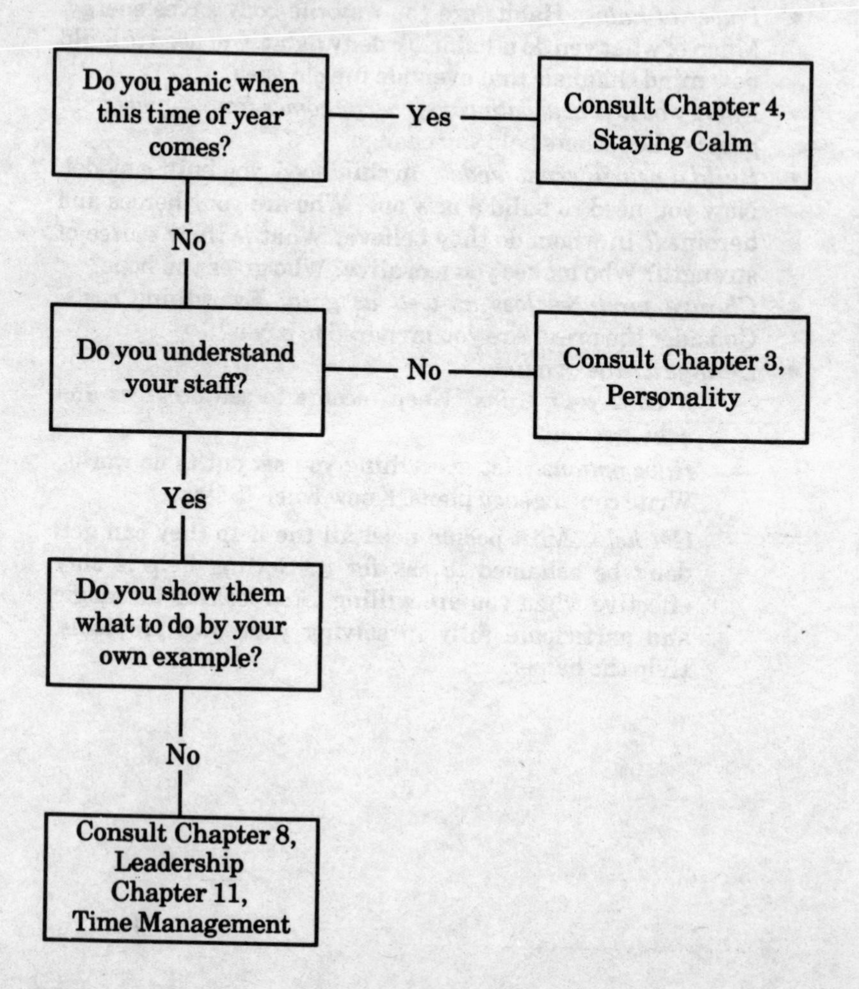

## Decision chart 2

Working in your office is like being in a zoo. No one seems to know where anything is and chaos reigns at all times.

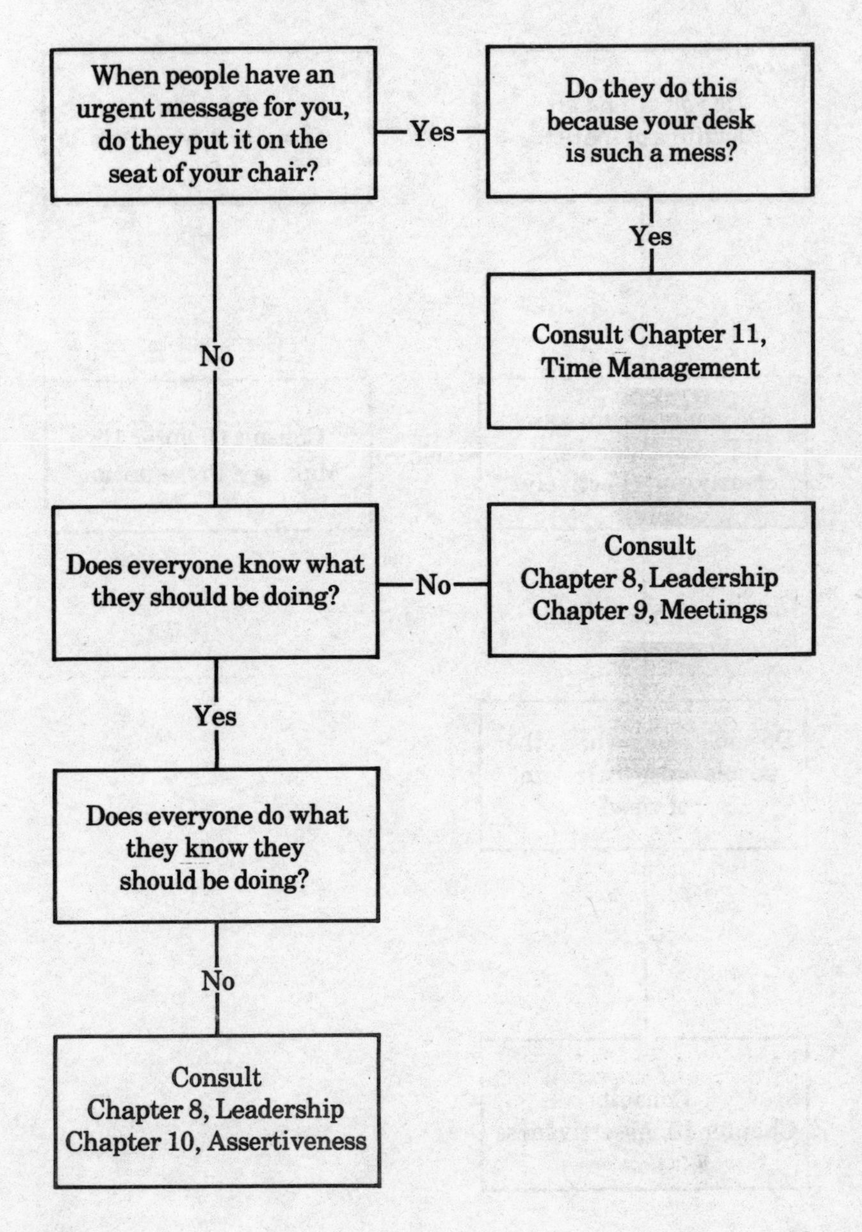

## Decision chart 3

When you are in discussion with other departments, they always seem to come out on top.

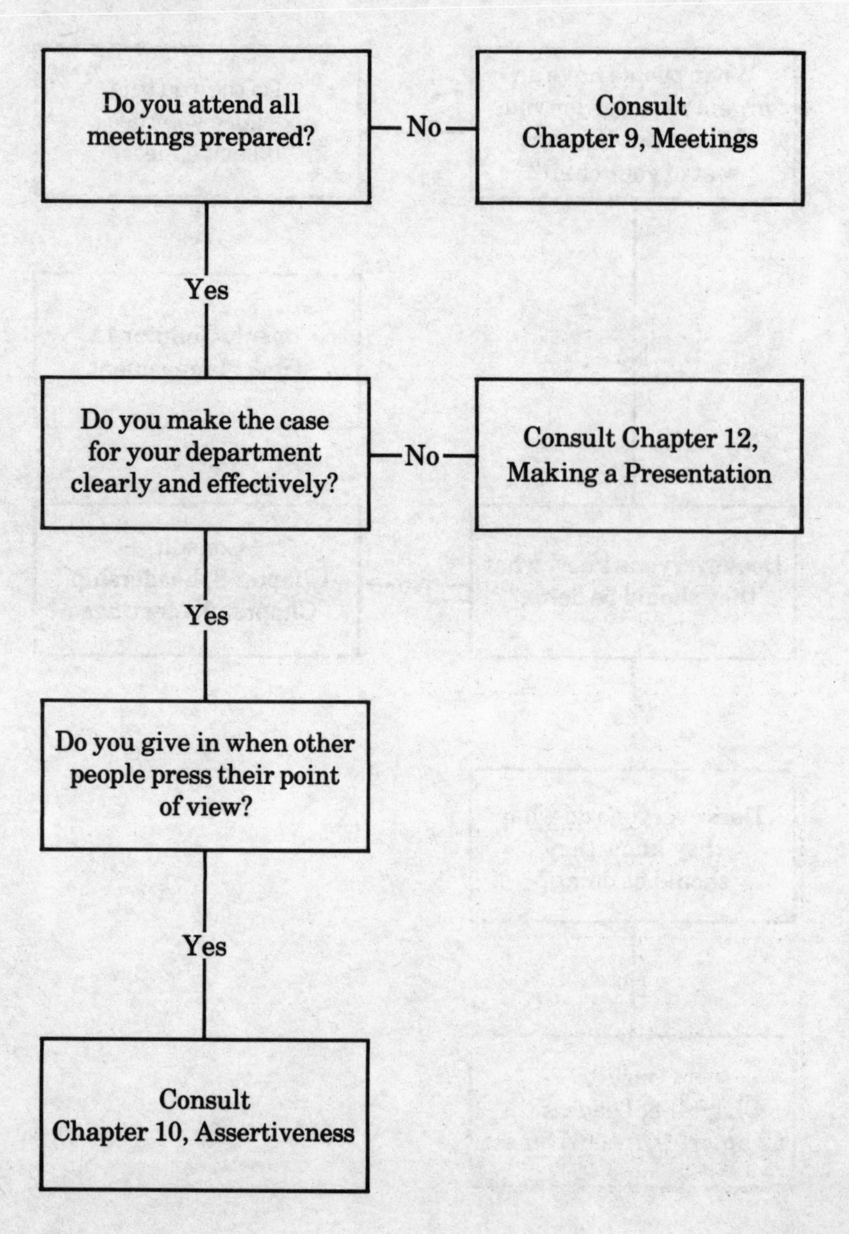

## Decision chart 4

Nothing ever seems to get done around here.

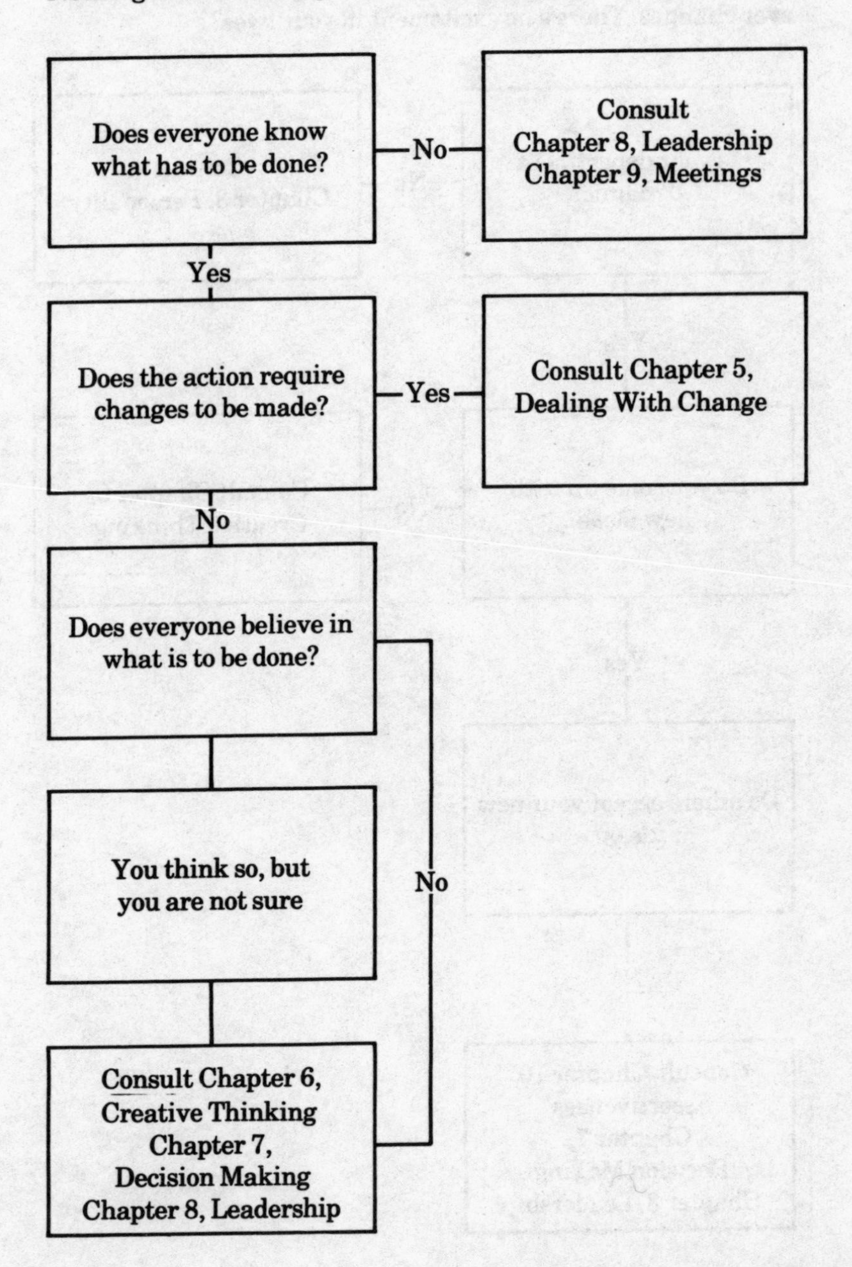

## Decision chart 5

Working in your department is like living in the past. Nothing ever changes. There's no excitement in your lives?

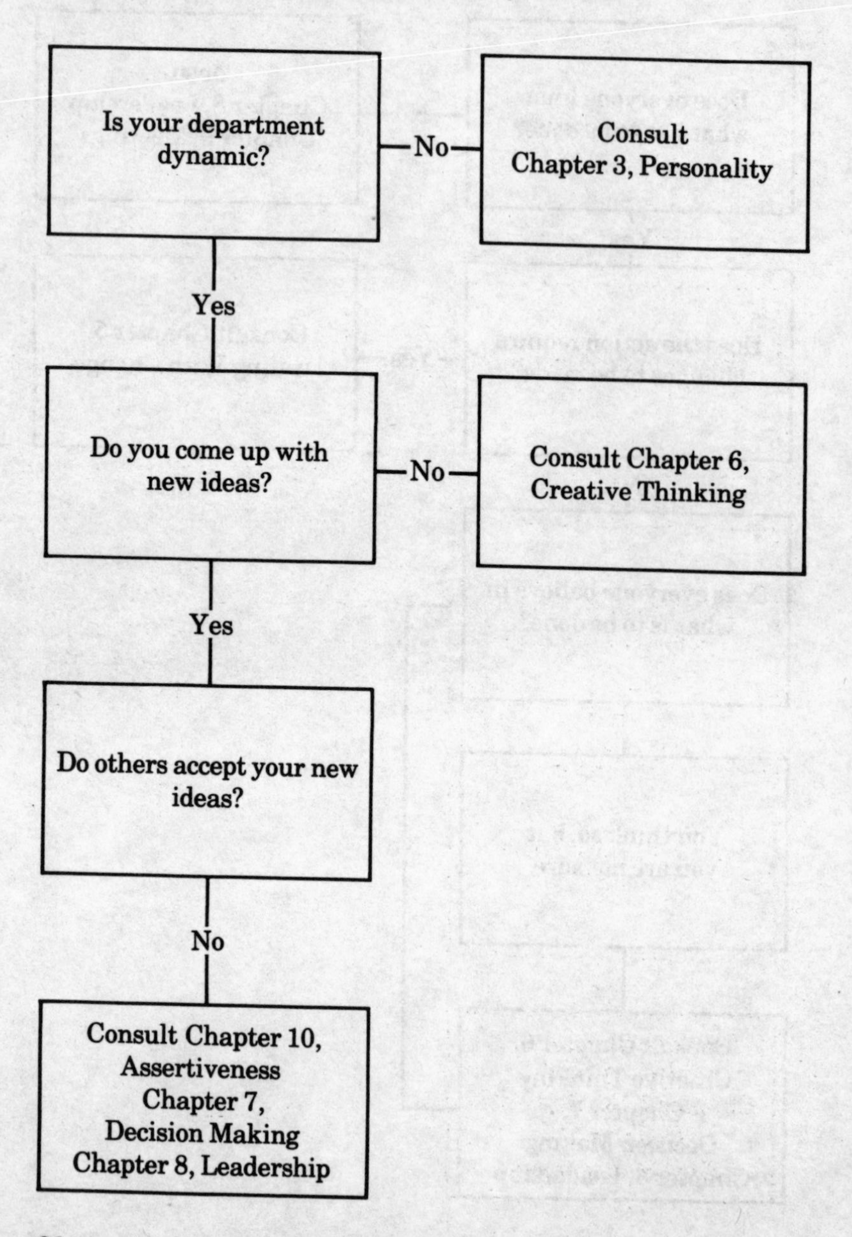

## Decision chart 6

It's all very well for other organisations, but you work for impossible people.

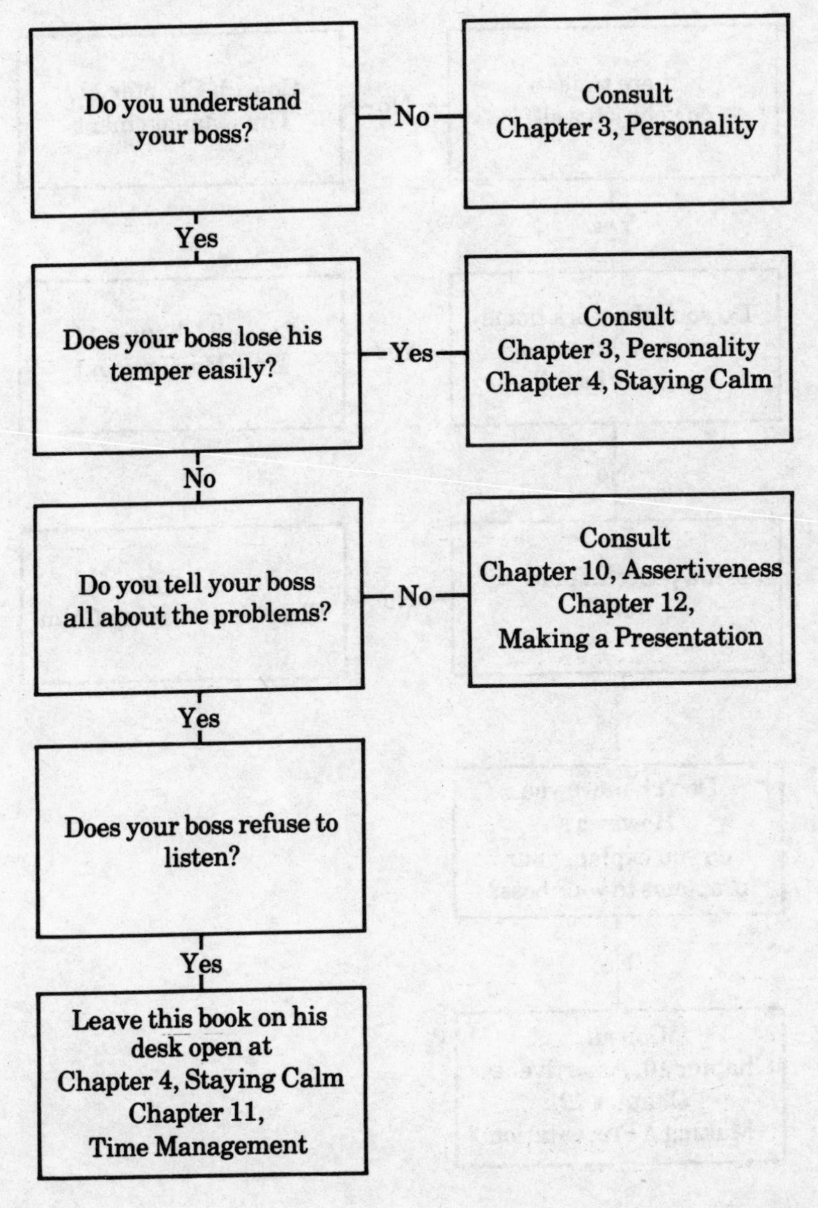

## Decision chart 7

These academic solutions are all very well, but you work in the real world and there just isn't time for all this messing about.

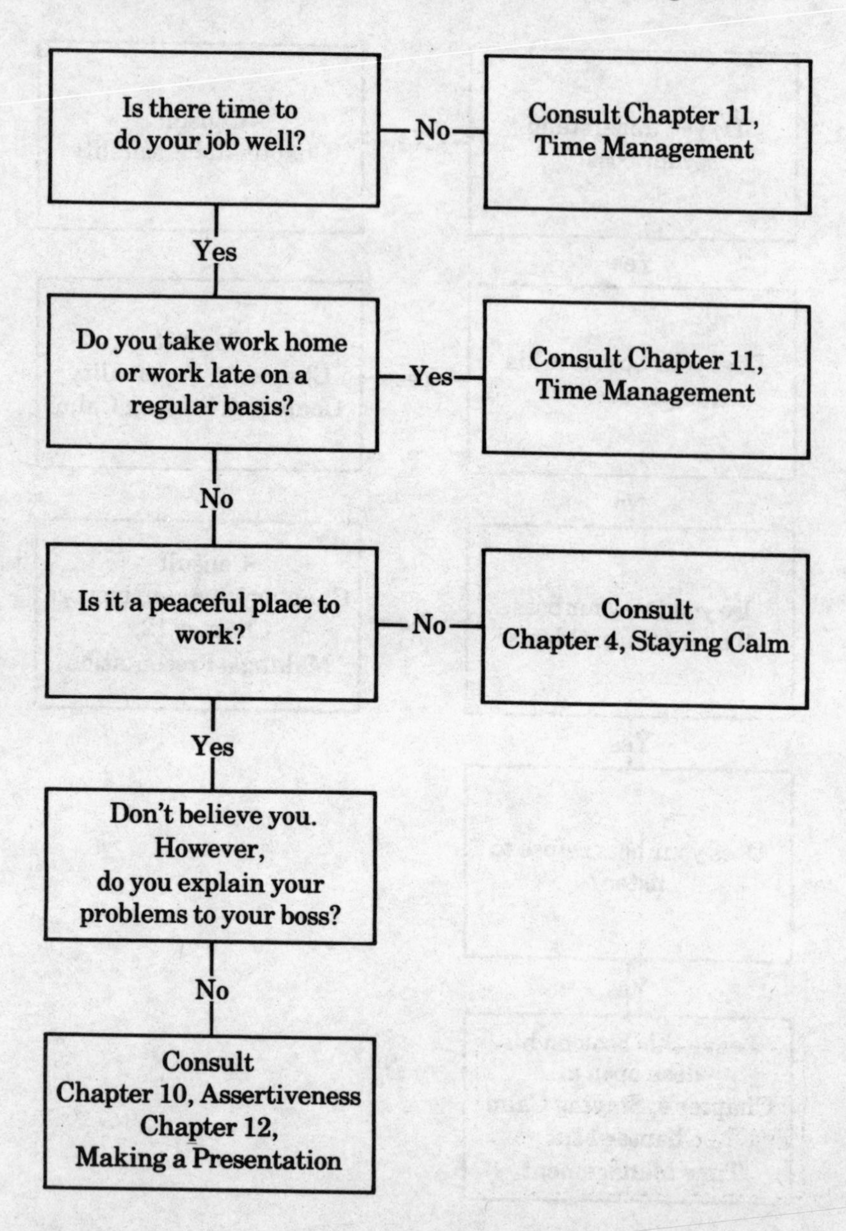

## Decision chart 8

You are here to do a job. You haven't got time for all these people and their petty problems.

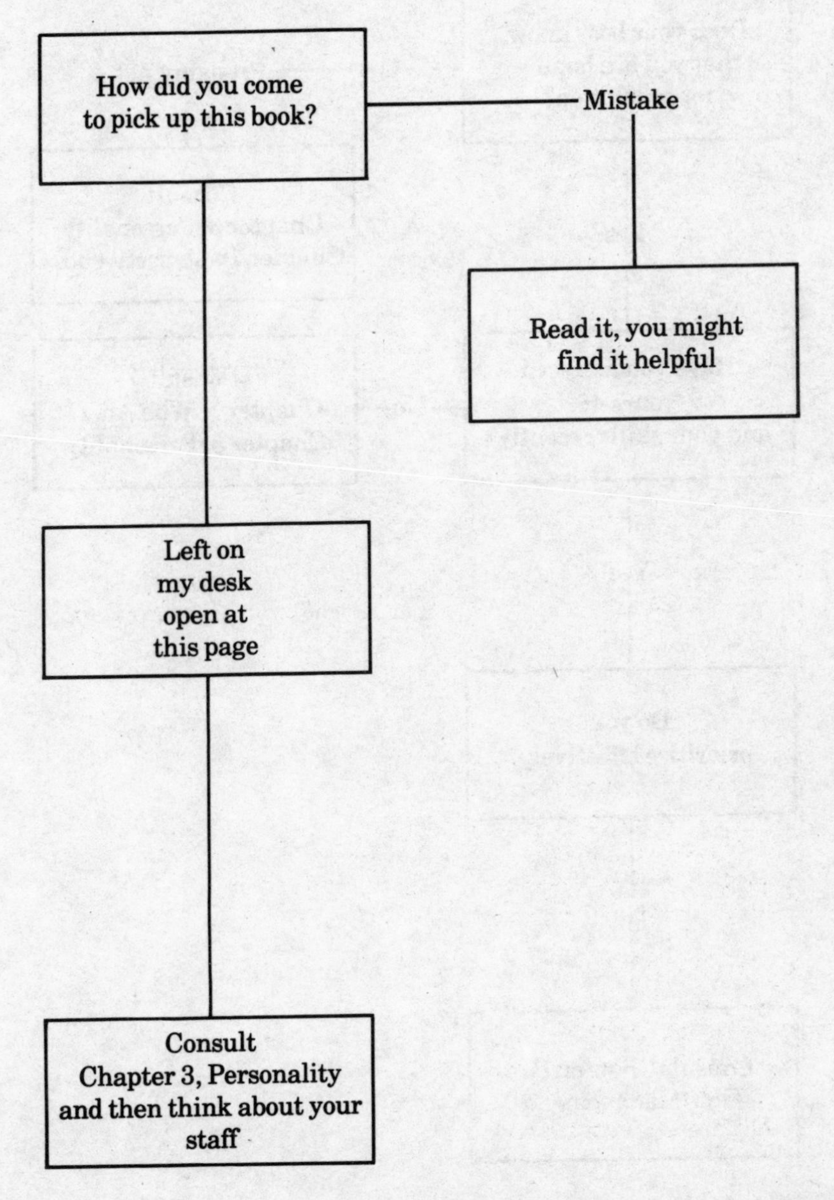

## Decision chart 9

You always seem to miss out on the promotion stakes.

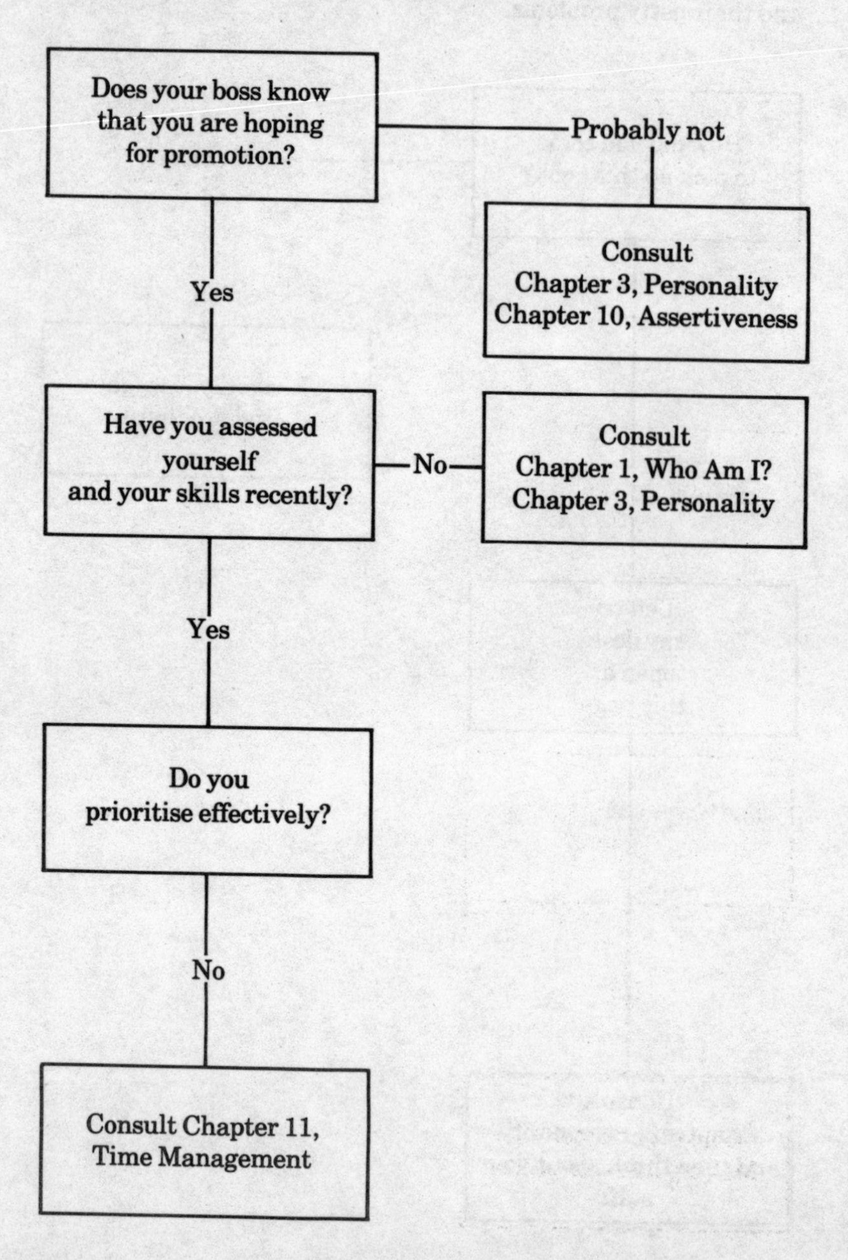

## Decision chart 10

Everything was all right until they tried to introduce the new system. Now people seem to have problems all the time.

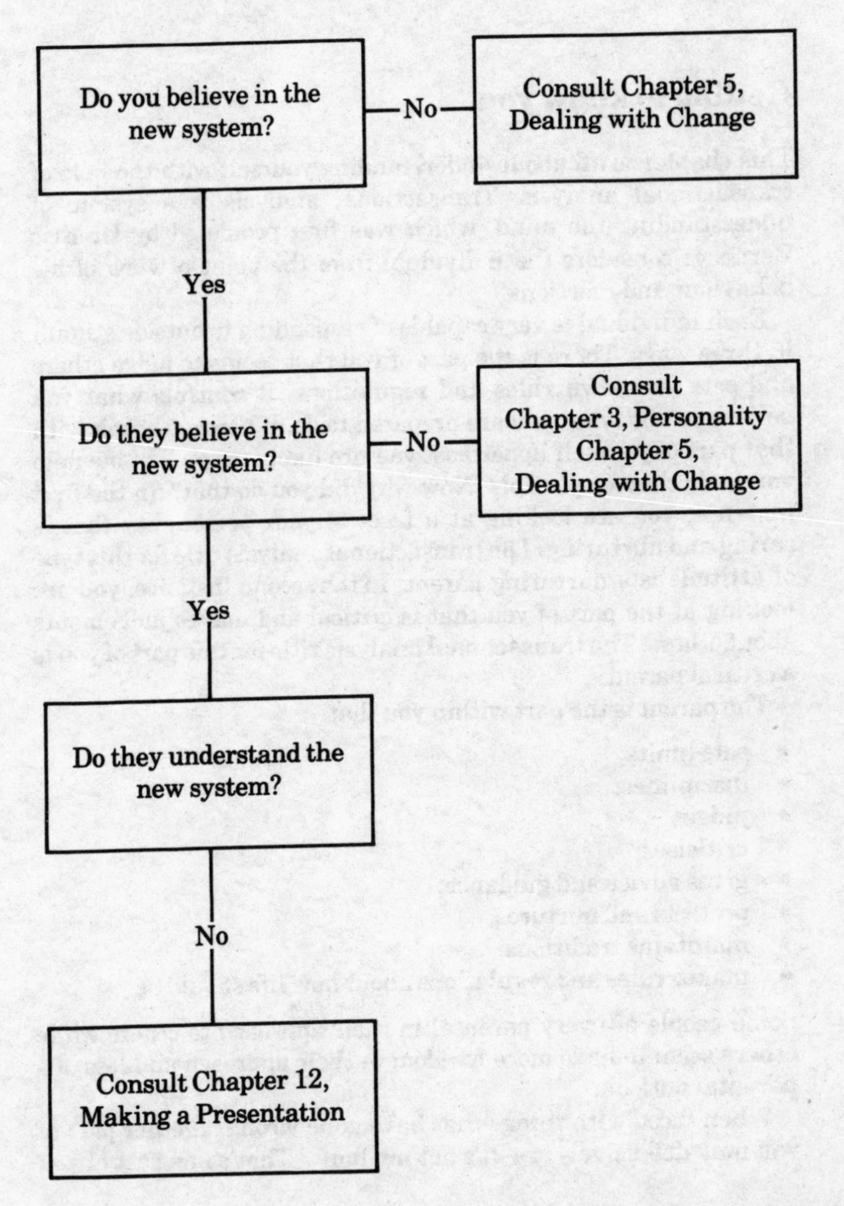

# *Chapter 3*
# Personality

## Getting to know you

This chapter is all about understanding yourself with the help of transactional analysis. Transactional analysis is a system of understanding the mind, which was first promoted by Dr Eric Berne. It considers the individual from the point of view of his behaviour and reactions.

Each individual is very capable of responding to outside stimuli in three ways. There is the part of you that seems to judge others and sets your own rules and regulations. It controls what you believe in and what you are prepared to do. When you speak with that part of yourself uppermost you are likely to say 'Let me help you to do that' or possibly 'Now why did you do that?' In the first instance, you are looking at a facet of your personality that is caring and nurturing. The transactional analysis title for this type of attitude is a nurturing parent. In the second instance, you are looking at the part of you that is critical and makes judgements about others. The transactional analysis title for this part of you is a critical parent.

The parent is the part within you that:

- sets limits;
- disciplines;
- judges;
- criticises;
- gives advice and guidance;
- protects and nurtures;
- maintains traditions;
- makes rules and regulations about how life should be.

Some people are very parental in their approach to others while others seem to have more freedom in their approach and less of a parental outlook.

When faced with things that have gone wrong, another part of you may defensively cry 'It's not my fault.' That same part of you responds with feelings and energy, creativity, curiosity and intuition, and reacts spontaneously to everything around you. This is the child within you. Every individual is capable of stamping his feet and sulking when faced with problems. Some people are capable too of being completely spontaneous and free in their responses. Most people, however, need alcohol or some other stimulant to bring out this free child approach. Each individual learns, during the course of his life, to adapt his child state into something that is acceptable to the world around him. Indeed, parents teach their offspring how to adapt this state and use it to get the attention they desire when they are small children. If you pause and think for a moment, you can probably think of plenty of business men who appear to be sitting in prams wearing their pinstripe suits waving their arms about in fury. In fact, every time they yell for a file or a cup of tea, it is as though they had thrown the rattle out of the pram and demanded that mother return it.

People are not entirely composed of parental and childlike attitudes. There is of course the logical, cool, calm and collected part of you that is capable of:

- gathering facts and data;
- sorting out the best alternatives;
- estimating probabilities;
- planning the steps in the decision-making process;
- asking questions.

This is the part of you that under transactional analysis is referred to as the adult ego state. Each individual is made up of a blend of three ego states with different mixes of parental and childlike approaches. To understand other people properly, you will need to identify the dominant ego state of anyone with whom you try to communicate. Identifying ego states is quite simple if you watch the body language and the words of the individual whom you wish to spot. Most individuals give themselves away by their behaviour and conversation.

Sometimes it is also possible to spot someone's behavioural state by the social impression they create upon you. People who make you feel small and appear patronising are nearly always dominantly parents while people who make you laugh and have fun are probably free children.

In addition, you can often spot ego states by realising that your feelings, at a particular moment in time, mirror those of your parents or relatives in the same situation. Perhaps this feeling can be best summarised by the saying 'Now I understand how my father felt when . . .'.

The final way of determining your ego state(s) is by self-analysis.

## Spotting your own ego state

### The critical parent

Looks angry or scowls whilst pointing a finger or thumping the table. Sneers or is angry or condescending. Is always critical. Takes a moralistic or superior attitude. Will be judgemental and an authoritarian, and always favours the hierarchy. Will not answer questions, refuses to give reasons and treats others as fools.

### The nurturing parent

Smiles a great deal and is warm, sympathetic and caring. Pats people on the back and encourages them. Takes a supportive, caring attitude. Tries to understand subordinates and is permissive. Adopts other people's problems as his own. Gives profuse praise.

### The adult

Is clear, calm, confident and of an enquiring nature. Appears relaxed, attentive and confident. Wears a smile and makes eye contact. Keeps an open mind, asks questions and is interested. Refrains from making judgements.

### The adapted child

Can be sulky or whiny. Can also be spiteful and taunt others. May be compliant or defiant; passive or complaining. The pattern of behaviour will be the one discovered to lead to the greatest rewards in childhood.

### The free child

Will show a great deal of energy with constantly changing behaviour. Fun loving and energetic; someone who lets feelings show. A spontaneous character who responds to others with clear intentions.

No *one* ego state is good or bad. The behaviour patterns of each of your reactions may be positive in the sense of having healthy, helpful and effective outcomes for relationships and work or negative in the sense of having unhealthy, destructive and damaging outcomes. Some people do, however, seem to rely on one ego state more than the others:

- Positive nurturing parent - cares for another person when that person needs or wants it.
- Negative nurturing parent - interferes and does things for others when they are not needed or wanted.
- Positive critical parent - is assertive.
- Negative critical parent - takes away the self-worth of another person.
- Positive adapted child - acceptable social behaviour
- Negative adapted child - self-destructive behaviour to get attention.
- Positive free child - has fun, creates and expresses thoughts freely.
- Negative free child - hurts self or others while having fun.

It's quite possible to compound your own feelings by holding a kind of internal dialogue:

> 'Oh, you are a fool' says your internal critical parent
> 'Yes I'm hopeless and miserable' replies your internal adapted child

If you do this too often, you remove the positive value of learning from mistakes and turn all mistakes into depressing effects.

Some people are constantly one type of individual and yet others contaminate their adult ego state with either parent or child reactions.

**The constant parent**

The constant parent will come across as either:

- a critical parent who is controlling, judgemental and authoritarian - someone who, although you may respect, you do not enjoy working for; or
- a nurturing parent who is smothering and so fussy that you never feel free to be yourself.

If you work for people who are constant parents, you will never seem to have the freedom, power or opportunities to develop problem-solving and decision-making skills.

### The constant adult

People who are in a constant state are very effective thinkers, planners and problem solvers. However, they seem to have no sense of humour and very often are totally uncommitted in debates about right and wrong. If you work for such an individual, you will develop and grow but you will not find life fun.

### The constant child

People who are constant children are usually charming, humorous, creative, impulsive and totally lacking in rational thinking, and often without well-defined social values. Such people are hard to predict and often extremely difficult to work for. They often behave like small children, stamping their feet and arguing at the first provocation.

### Contaminated egos

Contamination occurs when the parent or child ego states enter into the adult ego state. People who are in the adult ego state contaminated by the parent often hold tenacious, prejudice-based opinions which they refuse to update in the face of information from the outside world. Obviously, such prejudices act as barriers to communication and problem solving. Such people come across as bigots and appear determined to make others' lives miserable.

People whose adult ego state is contaminated by the child may often have delusions of either grandeur or inability. Very often, extreme stress causes managers to develop this contaminated ego state. Whatever the reason, the child-contaminated adult can be almost impossible to work for.

## Strokes

Stroking is a way of indicating to others how you feel about them. It doesn't need to be a physical reaction: it may simply be words of praise, but very often it involves touching as well. Positive strokes are the giving of praise while negative strokes are the giving of criticism.

Positive strokes can be given for two reasons. Merely for just being alive, as in 'I like you.' Here, 'I like you' is an unconditional stroke. More effectively, a positive stroke can be conditional upon the action carried out by the individual to be stroked, as in 'Well done, you completed that tasks exactly as I had hoped. I'm pleased with you.'

Negative strokes may be either conditional on actions or merely given because an individual is not liked. Where a negative stroke is conditional on actions, it at least has the merit of responding to something outside; where it is simply dislike for the individual being alive, it is singularly destructive.

In the mid-balance between positive and negative stroking is a no-stroke situation. As managers of people, it is always wise to rely on interest rather than to try to stimulate relationships, since you can never rely on liking everyone you have to deal with, but you can rely on being interested in everyone you meet. Interest becomes a positive stroke that is conditional on action and may indeed be interpreted as a positive stroke that is unconditional. The more the positive strokes you are prepared to give your staff, the more they will respond to a feeling of belonging and warmth. Some people have an imbalance in strokes, created from when they were young. If you received more negative strokes when you were young, the more your balance will veer towards the search for negative strokes. People who look for a certain type of stroke often build up a safety valve reservoir, so as to be able to correct any imbalance they experience. If you have a bias towards negative strokes from childhood, you will not be happy when you are praised a lot and you will deliberately search for faults to correct your apparent imbalance. This is sad, as it stops people accepting genuine praise. If you wish to motivate yourself or others, it is wise to use strokes to reward freely. Forget the past, look to today and be grateful for all the rewards that people are prepared to offer you. Never fail to use that wonderful, helpful and responsive phrase 'thank you.'

## Transactions

A transaction is a unit of social intercourse, consisting of a stimulus followed by a response. If a transaction is to continue, rather like a game of tennis, the stimulus itself has to engender a response, which will engender a further stimulus, which will continue to engender a further response. So, each transaction is made up of various strokes and units of recognition.

Some transactions are very simple; people speak to each other on the same wavelength. For example, one secretary says to another 'Oh dear, my boss is hopeless.' The other then replies 'Yes, my boss is too.' Both of these secretaries are discussing their bosses as though they were small children and are happily communicating parent to parent. There are nine possible complementary transactions but the most useful are the ones that remain on the same wavelength, as follows:

- parent speaks to parent - parent replies to parent
- adult speaks to adult - adult replies to adult
- child speaks to child - child replies to child.

The five other possible complementary transactions are:

- parent to adult - adult to parent
- parent to child - child to parent
- adult to parent - parent to adult
- child to adult - adult to child
- child to parent - parent to child

The latter complementary transactions are, however, less beneficial. If you speak to an individual in a patronising tone, you are likely to illicit a childlike response. This may be all well and good when you are dealing with a child, but highly unsatisfactory if you are expecting that adult to produce satisfactory work. For this reason, it is better to try to communicate on the same wavelength at all times.

**Crossed transactions**

Sometimes the adult speaks to another adult but gets the response of a child to a parent. For example, if you raise a query as to why a mistake has occurred, the response is not one of 'Oh dear, how can we put it right,' which would be the adult replying to the adult, but rather one of 'It's not my fault. I didn't do it,' which is the child replying to the parent. The temptation is to respond as a parent and say 'Well, as far as I can see, you did do it wrong.' Once you have got into parent/child and child/parent communication, it is less likely to be successful on a business level. There are four common crossed transactions:

- adult to adult - child to parent
- adult to adult - parent to child
- child to parent - adult to adult
- parent to child - adult to adult

Each of these common crossed transactions results in wavelengths being contaminated and probably hinders successful business communication. It is always wiser to stay in the adult-to-adult mode when working in the office.

### Complex transactions

A complex transaction involves the use of two ego states by either the instigator or the responder, or both. The least complicated of these is where a clear message is apparently transmitted but a hidden message is implied. For example, in adult-to-adult mode, you tell your boss that ABC Co have booked advertising space in the issue of a magazine. The implication that you are seeking for him to understand is that you cannot afford not to advertise in the magazine if your rivals are already doing so. This hidden message is really from the parent to the child. If the boss gets the strong hidden message, he is likely to respond 'Oh dear, have they, well we had better take some space too.' He is not responding adult to adult but instead is recognising the hidden parent/child message. This is a classic selling technique and one that relies on the greed and desires of the child.

Sometimes the crossed transactions are of a multi-mixed nature. For example, in the adult-to-adult message 'Come into my office, I'd like to have a word with you,' the hidden message is 'Come into my office and I'm going to tell you off for failing to get this job right.' The response, adult to adult, is 'OK, I'm on my way,' but the hidden response is 'I know I made a mess of the job and I'm in for a bollicking.' The problem with such hidden ulterior messages is that if they become commonly used within the working life, they will always be believed to be there in implied communication. It is better to speak clearly adult to adult and to make it clear, when you wish to tell someone off, that that is your purpose and intention, but be constructive in the way you announce your intention.

### Communication rules

It follows, in fact, that if you want to communicate clearly and effectively, you will need to apply the following rules:

- As long as transactions are complementary, communication may continue indefinitely.
- If there is a change to a crossed transaction, a break in the flow of communication is likely to occur. Once that break has occurred, something different may well happen afterwards.
- The outcome of any ulterior transactions will be determined at the psychological level of the individuals involved, and not at the ordinary level of social exchange.

## Relating to others - Life positions

If you understand why you say and do certain things, you can also see why you take certain fixed attitudes in life. These fixed attitudes are your life positions and explain how you see yourself in relation to others. There are four basic life positions.

**I'm OK, you're OK**
People occupying this life position are optimistic, happy and confident about work and life. They use time constructively, relate happily to their friends and contacts, and are assertive. These people are likely to succeed in life.

**I'm OK, you're not OK**
People in this life position hate others. The positions are characterised by feelings of anger, fury and hostility. Other people are seen as inferior, unworthy, incompetent, wrong and not to be trusted. People who take this life position tend to hold dogmatic views, believing theirs to be the only right course. They often devote time to putting others down and are highly competitive and aggressive with an enhanced view of their own self-worth. However good they believe themselves to be, these people are not successful in life.

**I'm not OK, you're OK**
People in this life position feel sad, inadequate, stupid or ugly. In business, they see themselves as powerless and inferior in relation to others. Such people put themselves down and find it difficult to accept positive strokes, often being suspicious of them. In life, in general, they don't succeed and are unhappy and depressed.

**I'm not OK, you're not OK**
People in this life position wonder where they are going. Why bother? What's the point? They are defeatist people who make no effort to change things. The defeatist does not succeed in life, and he may also cause others to fail too.

If people feel very strongly that they belong in a 'not OK' position, it tends to affect them adversely. 'I'm not OK, you're OK' may result in severe depression and illness, whereas 'I'm not OK, you're not OK' can lead to alcoholism or drug dependency. Most people do not experience long periods in the 'not OK' positions however. Most people move through the quartile of experiences as they move through time. The longer they spend in the 'I'm OK, you're OK' position, the happier their lives will be. It follows, therefore, that it is worthwhile trying to keep yourself in an 'I'm OK, you're OK' position. The way not to do this is to try to like other people. If you try to like other people, you are bound to fail with some. You are also bound to feel concerned about whether or not they like you. The secret to feeling OK with other people and accepting them with tolerance is to be interested in them. Whenever you meet someone new, become interested in them as a human being and use that interest to find out as much as you possibly can about them. The interest will come across as like and will enhance the ego of the person to whom you are talking. On the other hand, it will release you from the necessity of having to like someone and give you the freedom to relate to them as yourself.

## Time structuring

Time structuring is the way you choose to spend your life span between birth and death. There are six ways open to you:

- *Withdrawal* - no contact with others.
- *Rituals* - socially programmed exchanges, eg, 'Good morning, how are you?'
- *Pastimes* - superficial exchanges about non-threatening subjects, eg, sport.
- *Activity* - external goal-directed behaviour, eg, work and hobbies.
- *Games* - recurring transactions with concealed motivation.
- *Intimacy* - game-free honesty and openness, free of exploitation.

The preferred time structuring of an individual will be reflected in his/her management style:

- *Withdrawal* - someone who avoids contact with others and abdicates responsibility, as in 'More than my job's worth.'
- *Rituals* - someone who will only do things in a set order or according to the rule book. Often a very petty approach, as in 'Sorry, the rules say . . ., and that's how we'll continue to do it.'
- *Pastimes* - someone who worries more about what others will think than he does about the job he is doing, as in 'We can't possibly do that, what would the MD think?'

- *Activity* - someone who is more concerned for production than for the people involved, as in 'Come on, stop messing about and let's get on with it.'
- *Games* - someone who believes in his own way of doing things and does not like to change, as in 'I hear what you say, but let's stick to my way, we know that works.'
- *Intimacy* - a practitioner of human relations-based management.

Good management style needs a combination of all six time structures with no total dominance in just one structure.

## The game of life

People play games. Sometimes these games are called 'office politics'. They are, however, games that are designed to bring about favourite emotions or feelings. Once you start playing a game, you tend to continue, as such games are repetitive, predictable and likely to have an ulterior motive. If you enjoy playing a particular kind of game, perhaps being boss and making sure others suffer as a result, you will always seek weak people around you, so that you can play the game you prefer. In fact, most games seem to be designed to engender bad feelings in at least one of the parties involved. Because people play games with their lives, it explains why people tend to set out with good intentions of never making the same mistakes again, yet when they change their job or their life partner they end up making exactly the same mistakes.

Games are negative actions and normally they are used to engender bad feelings. People get into the habit of playing games without really being fully aware of what they are doing. The only way to stop playing games to to be aware of your attitude. Each individual probably has one or two favourite games of a type that suits his personality.

### Victim games

People who enjoy victim games are people who like feeling that they are to blame for something that has happened. It is an 'I'm not OK, you're OK' position. Some of the buzz words characteristic of these victim games are:

- I'm so bad . . . .
- The whole world is against me.

- I'm so stupid I can't understand anything.
- If it weren't for my . . . I could succeed.
- I always have to work so hard and be in such a rush.
- Misery loves company.
- There's always something to go wrong.
- It's not my fault.
- No one ever takes my advice.

### Persecutor games

Other people prefer to be the boss and the persecutor in games. These are the people who like to surround themselves with inadequate colleagues or people who will happily suffer as a result of their behaviour. The kind of games they play are best described by the following:

- I'm so superior I only had to wait for you to . . .
- Someone ought to put him down.
- I'm going to test your powers of tolerance by making lots and lots of mistakes.
- You're wrong whatever you do.
- You're wonderful . . . oh no you're not.
- You just can't win against me.
- Men/women are only after one thing.
- I can fault anything you do.

### Rescuer games

Finally, a third group of people like to be seen as the world's rescuers. These are the people who like a situation to crop up where one person is suffering at the hands of another so that they can appear to be the knight in shining armour who comes along to rescue the situation. Very often these people find themselves taken for granted or treated in a less than thankful manner. The kind of games they play are:

- You're incapable of . . .
- How could you be so ungrateful?
- I'm having a miserable time looking after everybody.
- If we make enough noise, we'll avoid actually having to do anything.

### Triangles

A drama triangle is formed by a pesecutor, rescuer and victim together playing a game of life. Most people tend to have a favourite role and seek that role at all times. However, you can switch in certain situations. By playing games, people can:

- avoid responsibility for their problems;
- avoid risks in being intimate;
- make people and situations predictable;
- exchange negative strokes;
- structure time predictably;
- re-experience a favourite bad feeling;
- confirm a life position;
- further their life plan.

## Life scripts

As a result of your background and upbringing, you develop preferences for certain games. They represent the roles you play each day. They are chosen to enhance your life scripts. A life script is the plan you make and set for yourself, deciding on it at a very early age according to your experiences of life. For healthy development, each individual also needs a series of permissions to help him develop his capabilities fully:

- *To exist* - to be cared for and loved and not to be ignored.
- *To feel sensations* - to feel hunger, pain, thirst, etc. and not to deny those feelings.
- *To feel feelings* - sad, mad, bad and scared and to feel them openly.
- *To think* - to read, solve problems and develop the adult ego state.
- *To be close to others* - to have physical contact.
- *To be the sex you are* - to relate correctly to the same sex parent.
- *To be the age you are* - to grow up.
- *To make it* - to develop without jealousy.

The presence or lack of these permissions, granted by your parents, will affect the life scripts you choose, which are as follow:

- *Winners:* The script that produces most positive strokes. Winners learn from experiences without punishing themselves with the critical parent. They have fun without hurting and have plenty of free child.
- *Non-winners:* The script that experiences an even distribution of positive and negative strokes. Most people are non-winners.

These people have their ups and downs and are often successful in life without enjoying that success to the full.

- *Losers:* The script that produces most negative strokes. People who seem to be on a hiding to nowhere, whose life turns into a battle with authority or the mind.
- *No love:* A no-love script is based on injunctions that limit stroking. Rules are: don't give strokes if you have to give them; don't ask for strokes when you need them; don't reject strokes when you don't want them; don't give yourself strokes; don't accept strokes if you want them. This script seems to affect more women than men.
- *No mind:* The child's intuition, emotions and rational thinking capabilities are discounted.
- *No joy:* Based on injunctions preventing people from enjoying their bodies and thus encouraging them to disregard their bodily sensations as being pleasant or unpleasant. It tends to produce dry, intellectual, rational people who may need to rely on stimulants for emotions.

You develop your life scripts by first recording and measuring early experiences: the way your parents treat you, how you get their attention, what people you are told to be like. Next, you make decisions about the world and it's relationship to you. Perhaps it is a warm, friendly place, maybe it is hard and cruel. Next, you think out the sort of person you are and link it with what happens to people like you. At this stage, role models are important.

Once you know what your script is to be, you set about structuring your time to give satisfacton to the script, and you indulge in games to reinforce that satisfaction. The payoff can range from a life of achievement to madness and sadness; from an ordinary life to one that is abnormal and disturbed; from being alone to being part of a relationship.

## Being the best person you can

'I'm OK, you're OK' is the most successful stance to adopt. But for that, you need to learn to like yourself. How can you do that?

- *Ego states:* The way to get the best out of your own ego state is to reduce any pompous or bigoted parent behaviour. It will also be essential to let your free child show and to let your emotions react to situations as they occur. Forget the ways you learned to attract attention in your youth and develop new ways that are more helpful and kind to others. Develop your adult state for business life and work in the adult as much as possible, resorting to natural child for humour and light relief. Never allow your ego state(s) to become contaminated or bigoted.

- *Strokes:* Say 'thank you' to people when they have done something nice, but don't merely stroke them for being alive. Smile at people and respond to them warmly. Remember behaviour breeds behaviour.
- *Transactions:* If you are aware of the effect your conversation and communication can have on others, then you will be able to concentrate on making that as helpful and supportive as possible. So the answer is to become aware of how you are sounding and what you are saying.
- *Life positions:* You are probably the best you will ever be and the people around you are the same, so spend some time thinking about how you're OK and they're OK.
- *Time structuring:* Spend more time in relationships and intimacy and avoid playing games with life. Increase your skills at pastiming. Leisure is one of the most important things available to you.
- *Games:* Don't play games and don't let others drag you into playing games. The outcome of games can be unhappiness and discomfort.
- *Life scripts:* Never allow yourself to accept a loser script. Change your non-winner approach at the personal or organisational level to a winner script. Remember the winner does not always come first, but he knows that when he has come second he has given his best performance.

Awareness is the key to handling and stopping games: if you know yourself and how you predictably react; stop yourself and think before reacting. Adult behaviour is not involved in games. Putting the adult into the ego state will control games.

*To cure yourself:*

- analyse why you felt bad;
- plan a different approach for next time.

*Reduce your involvement by:*

- declining to put yourself and others down;
- declining to exaggerate strengths and weaknesses;

- refusing to move into persecutor or victim position;
- exchanging genuine positive strokes;
- spending more time in activity and intimacy.

Remember: *Where there's life there's hope.* You can always change if you actually want to. Wanting to change means with every part of you. Man is pro-active and not reactive. You don't have to play the roles others set for you. You can reject them and set your own life. You do not have to be the person your parents wanted you to become; you can be your own person, if you want to. Wanting means wanting with every ego state.

Take care of yourself and like yourself. How can you expect others to like you if you do not like yourself? You are ultimately responsible for your own feelings and behaviour. Never let someone else make you angry or sad. If you wish to be angry, let it be at your own choice; sad when you wish to and happy if you prefer. Do not be led by transactions into predestined games that force you to play a role in someone else's life script. If you choose to play that role yourself, then you have the freedom to quit or stay.

*Chapter 4*

# Staying Calm

## Introduction

Staying calm is easier said than done. The reason is simple: in dealing with management, you are dealing with people, and people are very frustrating. They do and say things that make you mad and then you react with anger and frustration. Frustration breeds behavioural changes, which in turn result in even more frustrating outcomes, and so a crisis or conflict emerges from a simple management situation.

The opposite to staying calm is becoming angry. Anger is an emotion and as such is seated in the child within you. Reacting with anger is reacting as a child. Reacting with anger to another already angry person is one child fighting with another. Staying calm despite the provocation is being an adult. Not only is it a more productive state, but also it helps to stop the anger from the other person.

Sometimes the anger is not directed at others but rather at the stupidity of an action that you yourself have taken. The solution is just the same: fight inward anger with more anger and all you have is a very angry person indeed, one who is likely to do something really stupid. Fight inward anger with calm reason and the adult takes over.

## How to make yourself angry

The major fact you have to realise is that no one else ever made you angry; you made yourself angry. Anger is a simple reaction to an outside stimulus, as illustrated by the following:

1. You want something. Step one to getting angry begins with wanting. Obviously, not all wanting leads to anger.
2. You failed to get what you wanted. Now you are frustrated. It is the failed wants that take you further on the road to anger. Frustration is not anger, however. It is what you do about the frustration that determines the outcome.

3. It is awful and very wrong not to get what you want. Now the frustration has been defined as a major catastrophe. The route to anger, depression, fear or hate is opening up. Still, you have the choice and the outcome may be depression if you feel a failure as a result of the frustration. Upsetting thoughts cause you to behave in an upset manner.
4. 'You should not frustrate me. I must have my own way.' This is the point at which anger takes the lead. A dictatorial attitude leads the frustration into anger.
5. 'You are a bad person for frustrating me.' Now hate and thoughts of revenge begin to lead the way.
6. 'Bad people should be punished.' The final step in the route to anger. The anger will not stop until you have inflicted pain on some other person.

The route to anger is paved with opportunities to avoid the final angry outcome, as follows:

- Wanting is part of achieving, but wanting must be achievable and possible.
- Frustration can avoid anger if you take it as an opportunity to examine why the preferred outcome was not reached and how future results can be improved.
- It is not terrible to fail. Failure is an opportunity to learn a better way. Failure is a positive thing. You can reverse failure by learning from it, not by compounding it with anger.
- 'No one frustrated me, I frustrated myself. Perhaps your behaviour caused me to frustrate myself, but I can hardly blame you for that.'
- People are not their actions, they are themselves despite their actions. It is possible to prefer one approach without rejecting another as bad.
- Inflicting punishment and pain causes a desire for revenge and thus the conflict cycle continues. Treating people badly simply convinces them to continue to behave badly. Recognising the positive possibilities of their behaviour helps them to see these too.

## Anger is getting things out of proportion

### Annoyance versus crisis

Anger comes about because you see frustrations as major disturbances. On the contrary, most frustrations are quite tolerable. Indeed, they can be turned into the stimuli that allow you to make even greater successes as a result of minor failures. Ask yourself some simple questions to get the frustration into proportion:

- Will they shoot my dog for this?
- Has anyone burnt the house down?
- Will I go to gaol?
- Has the world ended?

If the answers are no, then you may well have got the initial frustration out of proportion.

### The relationships between anger and fear

Anger can be a cover for fear. The cornered animal attacks because it is afraid. Sometimes when you are corrected for a mistake, you see the correction as an attack on your failure and begin to fear for your continued ability to do the job.

Angry people are often the most scared and the most inadequate. They simply become violent to save them facing the truth. To help them, the truth must be presented in a way that removes all fear.

### The relationship between self-pity and anger

Self-pity is one of the ways to depress yourself. An alternative behaviour pattern, when faced with the statement that it is wrong and bad to be frustrated, is depression and self-blame. Anger at this point is avoided, but the feelings are equally strong. The build-up of self-pity over the years can suddenly lead to an abrupt change. The worm turns; anger is the result. Anger and self-pity are triggered by the same behaviour pattern.

### Self-importance and a dictatorial attitude

Dictators are people who know that they are right and thus anyone who does not agree with them is wrong. They think that those who are wrong are bad and should be punished. Angry people are dictators for the period of their anger. You can even recognise the patterns of thinking: 'Yes, we are important; each of us is important. Yes, we must believe in ourselves if we are to succeed, but not at the cost of the destruction of others. I'm OK, you're OK.'

**Righteous anger**
All anger is 'technically' righteous, since the act of being angry is the belief that you are right and someone else is wrong. So there is no justification in being morally right.

## Blame

Blame is central to all anger:

The child says: 'It's not my fault.'
The critical parent says: 'What have you done, you stupid person?'
The adult says: 'How can we learn from this situation?'

It is blame that leads to an unfair outcome, in that an individual is singled out, to bear all the responsibility. But blame is not responsibility. To distinguish blame from responsibility, you have to separate the actions from the person. Allocating blame and destroying the person in the process is a waste of time. It is far better to spend the time correcting the situation as it now stands, and best of all to learn from the event.

**Forgive the act, learn the lesson**
The real way to avoid blame is to forgive the event but remember the outcome and what you learned as a result of it. If you forgive the event, you stop nagging and worrying about it. It ceases to be a viper at your bosom. If you remember the lesson, you stop yourself repeating the situation that led to the blame in the first place.

**The more you blame them, the worse they get**
Indeed, the more you blame other people, the worse they get at the task you are blaming them for. By allocating blame, you teach other people to hate themselves and to become depressed. You give them levels of performance that suggest they are failures. If you keep blaming them, they will feel there is no way out; they will cease to try to improve. As a consequence, you will inevitably begin to hate them, because they are bad at their job and so cause you frustration, and thus anger perpetuates itself when blame is involved.

**A pessimist is never disappointed**
If you think the outcome will be failure, it usually is. Self-fulfilling prophecies come about because, by your attitude, you make them come true. Believing that people do not want to work and that they

are thoroughly lazy will make them feed that that is what you expect of them. They'll reward you with the satisfaction of being right. Letting people see that you believe they are capable of greater things and that you expect good performance will have them trying to live up to your beliefs.

**Blame is unfair**
When you blame someone for a failure, you are failing too. Your failure is as bad as theirs, as you have not seen the opportunity to learn from the problems.

## The effects of anger

Anger can have many effects: It

- increases your frustrations;
- prevents you from solving your problems;
- makes you a poor role model for others to copy;
- leads to even more anger as the cycle of internal conflict continues;
- makes other people angry too;
- can even make you physically ill.

Anger is not assertiveness (see Chapter 10). In fact, it is the enemy of assertiveness, because it detracts from the message being presented. At times, it seems to gain great respect. When it fails to gain respect, its reward is fear. Management by fear does not succeed for long. Instead, it breeds anarchy and revolt.

There are some fact to remember about anger:

- People do not always learn from past experiences. They repeat the same mistakes again and again until they learn how to change.
- You can change, provided you want to. It does not take time to change, just a total desire to change.
- You do not have to get angry just because others are angry. It is always possible to stay calm.
- By the example of your own behaviour, you can prevent anger entirely.
- Fighting anger with anger only results in twice as much anger.
- Such behaviour patterns are not all the fault of your parents or upbringing. You can make your own changes to your life

pattern if you wish. However, some people get angry just for the sheer enjoyment of the feeling.

## How to get rid of anger

- Control your own anger, if necessary by displacement. Break a match, stamp your foot or hit the wall in the seclusion of your own office to get the tension out of yourself.
- Believe that everyone can control anger and go on believing it. Look for the signs of the adult in both parties.
- Behaviour breeds behaviour. You can trigger the other person into anger by your own behaviour. If you ignore a customer, he will feel frustrated and frustration will lead to anger. If you acknowledge him and tell him you will be able to deal with him shortly, he will wait patiently.
- Use all your body language to express the pleasant. Smile as you speak. Look interested. Match your body language to your words.
- Watch out for the signs that someone is trying to take over the conversation and turn it into anger. Don't be led by the child into anger. Stay in the adult.
- Where there is an accusation, apply logic and analyse the facts. Stick to the facts at all times and keep opinion to one side.
- Listen to angry people. If you interrupt them, they take the time that you are speaking to get ready for another tirade.
- Be fair at all times. Face the facts and express them clearly.
- Teach people everything you have learned from the situation. Show them how they can learn too. Emphasise the positive side.
- Never forget that most people lack self-confidence. They are always ready to believe the worst and to see themselves under attack. Give them the benefit of the doubt and make sure that your meanings and intent are clear.
- Count to ten before you speak. It works.
- Laughter calms many situations. Don't use it to make the angry person seem a fool; try to get him to laugh with you over some aspect of the situation. Laughter will deflate the most stressful situation.

*Chapter 5*

# Dealing with Change

## Planning for change and development

There are only two things that you can be sure of when planning change: first, that it will please none of the people for at least the first half of the time and, second, that if you wish to go forward you will have to introduce it sooner rather than later. Reaslistic management needs to learn how to introduce change, which involves seeking the answer to questions like: What is the reason behind the fear of change? What makes the ordinary, sensible human being metaphorically dig a trench and refuse to budge when faced with the most straightforward changes?

### Uncertainty

Within the organisation, uncertainty caused by a change in the way things are done has the effect of confusion and disorientating the work-force. What the human animal doesn't know, it tends to fear; what it fears, it fights. Introducing change means educating for change, telling people well in advance of events all the details of what is to happen, and how it will affect them and their roles within the organisation. It also means coming clean if the effect is likely to be less than good.

### Loss of control

Change means just that; no more detailed knowledge of the system, no role of sage or adviser, just one more person trying to find out how to fit into the new order. Suddenly things are being 'done to' individuals rather than 'done by' them. Suddenly they are no longer in control of the situation or, apparently, their own destiny. The solution is simple: thwart the change at every turn; reinstate the old order for as long as possible. The only way round the resistance is to involve people in the decision making behind the change. Those with a hand in the design have a heart in the introduction of the new.

## Capability

Only the professional clowns like to look foolish; the remainder of the human race will do almost anything to avoid such a situation. That's the trouble with falling over: it's not the pain, it's the humiliation, the statement of human failure, the lack of capability to cope. Even the most ardent optimist has secret fears of capability and when it comes to change even the most capable individual feels vulnerable. The only solution is training: training in advance of the introduction of the change; training in the detailed scope of the new systems: morale boosting, highly motivational training that shows the individual not only that he can cope but also that he is totally capable of handling all that the organisation can throw his way.

## The grapevine

'What does it all really mean? They are telling us this, but is there something hidden that they won't let us know until it is too late?' The ripples of dissatisfaction can spread even faster than those resulting from a pebble thrown into a pool. Caused often by fear or loss of face, or the loss of something even more important - the job itself - grapevine rumours are very hard to silence. The only real solution is not to let them start up in the first place, and that means communicating all the way down the line, directly and clearly, to every member of staff to be affected by the change. It means effective personal communication; face-to-face presentations geared to explain, advise and inform.

## More work

Change always means more work, if only at the start to ensure that the new system is fully understood. It is also likely to mean more work for a long time, if not for ever. People don't object to that provided the division of labour is fair and everyone knows the new system and job responsibilities. More work can be sold with more benefits: job satisfaction, responsibility, authority, remuneration. But at all costs the facts must not be glossed over. Everyone must know the new systems and see them to be fair and equitable. If the reporting structure is to change, everyone needs to know all there is to know, how the changes will affect them personally and the potential benefits of the new structure. Once again, the watchword is communicate; inform people at every turn; over-inform them if necessary, but make sure that they know enough.

### The inevitable

Sometimes the change will be for the worse. If that is the case, hiding it will only make the outcome worse too. The truth can save a large number of difficult situations. People who know how bad things may become respond to the needs placed upon them. They leave and let the organisation cope without them or they put shoulder to the wheel and enjoy being important or indispensable. Either way they help the organisation.

### The element of surprise

'Have I got a surprise for you' sounds wonderful until you are the individual on the receiving end of the surprise. Even positive surprises need advanced warning. It takes time to adjust to understanding the elements of change. Impromptu speeches are always better for a little forethought and planning, as are impromptu reactions. If you want favourable reactions to change, you need to give advanced warning of the future events. All businesses need good planning; unexpected rises in sales are just as great a potential for disaster as unexpected falls. Plan for change, inform all the way, and watch out for the unexpected.

## Working with change

If it is accepted that change is essential in the developing organisation, then it is equally essential to find a way of making it at least acceptable to the majority of the work-force and preferably to make it desirable to all. There are some golden rules:

- *Over-inform people:* Tell them so much at regular intervals that they begin to be bored. Give them hand-outs or written instructions, make presentations, call meetings, talk to them and listen to their responses.
- *Brief people in groups:* By doing that, you tell the same group the same story. It is too easy otherwise to forget something or expand on one point in answer to a question.
- *Always take questions:* If you can't answer them, ask for time; if you can, do so. Questions are merely feedback and while the staff are talking to you they are not panicking in a corner.
- *Believe in what you tell them:* It is far too difficult to deceive people if you don't believe what you are saying. Somehow your body language, your words or your tone will show your own mistrust in your own words.

- *Use every opportunity to train people:* If change means new advances and advantages, then the edge is taken off the anguish.

## Action planning

Change is a particular example of the need to use effective action planning. The action planning cycle involves the following steps:

1. Identify the need.
2. Plan the action.
3. Review the progress.

To be effective, the action planning cycle needs to go on and on.

### Action planning checklist

*What is the need? Identify the need:*

- To improve openness.
- To develop a more effective form of leadership.
- To improve decision-making ability.
- To clarify objectives.
- Generally to review and improve the operation of the team.

*Agree the need with those affected. Agree the need:*

- Has everyone been consulted?
- Is there total commitment?
- Is more time needed to agree needs?

*To whom does the action apply? Involve the right people:*

- The whole team?
- Leaders of different teams?
- Task groups?
- An individual?

*How will you know if you have been successful? Assess:*

- Have development objectives been accurately defined?
- Are they measurable?
- Can other people help you to evaluate?
- What behavioural changes to you expect?

*Is anyone else likely to be affected? Consider other implications:*

- Other teams or departments?
- The organisation as a whole?
- Other team leaders?
- Do you need approval?

*What methods, techniques or actions need to be adopted? Use the right resources:*

- Action-centred leadership.
- What is the right management style for the situation?

*What other resources will be needed? Consider other implications:*

- Are you competent to undertake the task?
- Is external help needed?
- Can other work teams help?

*What time scale should be adopted? Get timings right:*

- Month?
- Year?
- Weeks?

*What system of progress review should be used? Results are used as a basis for further improvement:*

- Self-review?
- Process observation?
- Regular specific review meetings?

*How can you assess what further action is necessary? Results are used as a basis for further improvement:*

- Should you evaluate your effect on others?
- Should you analyse your needs again?

# *Chapter 6*
# Creative Thinking

## Thinking

Thinking is essential to all activities. Most thinking of this kind needs to follow trained and logical patterns. Sometimes logical and predictable thinking is not enough. When that time comes, you need to make your brain creative. This is not difficult: it just means using that half of the brain that most people ignore.

Logic is situated in the left-hand side of the brain and drives the right-hand side of the body; creativity is situated in the right-hand side of the brain and drives the left-hand side of the body. Quite commonly, creative people show this by writing with their left hands.

During logical thinking, the problem is fed into the brain through the eyes or ears and the problem-solving patterns are already awaiting it. Next, the logical section of the brain compares the problem with past experience and knowledge and the brain suggests the answer. Here are some facts about logical thinking:

- Logical thinking chooses between one thing and another. It is a binary system. A right or wrong answer will come forth. The best way of looking at things is the right way of looking at things and vice versa.
- Logical thinking must be right at every stage. Each step must be fully justified and lead to the next step. Each step must be correct for the lead to take place.
- Logical thinking is analytical. It needs to know where the idea came from; what the background to the idea is. It tries to find reasons to reject an idea, to eliminate the ideas one by one so as to arrive at the solution.
- The stages of logical thinking follow one from another in order. One stage has to be completed in order to reach the next. There has to be a reason for saying or doing something before it is said or done. Any gaps in the system mean discomfort and a concern to pause and fill them.

- Logical thinking concentrates on the relevance of the thoughts. Anything that is not relevant is rejected.
- Logical thinking moves in the most predictable direction. It seeks proof all the time and proof comes from following well worn and proven patterns. There is no reason to seek out new ideas in logical thinking until the old ones have shown themselves unable to help.
- Logical thinking is a closed procedure. The end product of logical thinking is to produce an answer.

For all these reasons, logical thinking is right for 95 per cent of thinking situations. If you are to succeed in 100 per cent of thinking situations, logical thinking needs to be backed up by creative thinking. On its own, logical thinking is wrong and restrictive in 5 per cent of thinking situations.

Creative thinking is the art of deliberately breaking with convention and forcing to the forefront the creative side of the brain. Here are some facts about creative thinking.

- Creative thinking changes. It employs change for the sake of change. No solution is considered perfect; there must always be the chance of a better solution. Creative thinking keeps an open mind.
- Creative thinking has no rights and wrongs. It is not looking for what is right, but rather for what is different. Creative thinking avoids yes and no.
- Creative thinking uses information to set off new ideas and new thoughts. Every idea, even if it is not workable in its present form, is examined to see what use can be made of it. Nothing is rejected out of hand. The creative thinker never looks to see why an idea is wrong, but rather what use can be made of the idea.
- Creative thinking encourages the use of jumps. The thinker is not restricted to a logical sequence. The jumps in creative thinking are unjustifiable until after they have been made. They are made for the sake of making them. Gaps are created for the same reason. Gaps may cause the thinker to look anew at an old problem, so they are deliberately created.
- Creative thinking is not restricted by the relevance or irrelevance of a thought. An intrusion to the thinking process is welcomed since it forces change, and from change comes new ideas. At all times, creative thinking seeks to avoid the obvious.

- Creative thinking accepts no boundaries. There is nothing to be lost by going beyond the problem in order to think about the problem.
- Creative thinking is completely open ended. The thinker may come up with a brilliant solution or no solution at all. The answer may come a long time after the thinking process is apparently over. No solution can be forced.

For these reasons, creative thinking is essential in 5 per cent of thinking situations. If you let it, it is capable of solving old problems. Creative thinking keeps the mind open at all times.

**The traps of logical thinking**

At times, it is extremely difficult to get away from logical thinking. Logical thinking relies on a network of memories and thought traces which form patterns in the mind. The brain remembers past experiences and channels thought along the same paths, using tried and tested patterns to achieve tried and tested solution. The resulting patterns are safe and have several advantages:

- *They are selective:* The mind is surrounded by a mass of information; patterns ensure that the processes selected are relevant. They form a recognised starting grid. They save time in considering where the thought process should begin.
- *They act as triggers:* Recognition of familiar events causes the brain to set up patterns of memory, thus saving time in repeating essential research to arrive at a solution.
- *They can act in code:* There is no need to repeat long processes of thought; the pattern will take for granted that the thought has taken place and pass to the next stage. Many stages in thinking can be coded in this way and need not be repeated.
- *They allow anticipation:* Experience shows that $X$ leads to $Y$, thus it can be assumed that $Y$ will follow $A$, if $A$ leads to $X$.
- *They map the environment of the thinker:* Patterns record past thought and the processes that were used. As such, they map the experiences that went into that thought.
- *They attribute labels and values to thoughts:* Past experience shows that $A$ is good and $B$ is bad. Thus, the pattern can short circuit the thinking process by attributing such values to a trigger word. If an employee has made a mistake in the past, the incident itself does not need to be remembered in detail; merely the name of the employee will be sufficient to give the information that is needed.

Such patterns, on the other hand, also have disadvantages, which serve to trap the thinker and prevent new ideas emerging:

- *They do not permit choice:* The paths of thought commonly used are so well trodden that they discourage the search for new routes. They prevent the changing of opinions and give rise to the charge of obstinacy.
- *Patterns rely on what is right and what is wrong:* It is not possible to change your mind nor to take a non-committal view.
- *They are so clear that it is impossible to change:* The wide, open route of thinking causes the thinker to go too fast to be side-tracked. The thinker has no choice but to follow the pattern to the bitter end.
- *They restrict change:* It is difficult to cut across patterns; once established, they continue in their own path. It is easier to establish a new pattern and link it to the old than it is to cut across the old and establish a new branch.
- *They get larger and larger:* With use, the path of the pattern grows, making it more and more dominant and less and less susceptible to change.
- *They polarise:* Patterns tend to establish themselves at the strong ends of the spectrum; thus it is easier to have two strong opposing patterns than several related ones. The related ones will all combine to give the strongest.
- *They grow by extension:* The use of the same pattern for different thoughts mean that the pattern not only gets more and more entrenched but that it also gets longer, in order to deal with the greater number of variances in the problems passing through it.
- *They lead to assumptions:* It is very easy to make an assumption when following a standard pattern. If the assumption is wrong, then the answer is wrong in part at least.
- *They reduce the meaning:* The frequent use of one pattern means that the triggers are such that there is no longer any need to consider the individual meaning.
- *They encourage mistakes:* It is very easy to follow the wrong pattern having made the wrong assumption or reacted to the wrong trigger.
- *They allow the wrong pattern to be selected:* Existing patterns may be inappropriate for the problems to be solved, yet the tendency is to search existing patterns before trying

something new.

- *They can cause difficulty in prediction:* The same trigger may produce a different answer from various people, simply because the patterns have been set by different experiences.
- *They require sequence:* Unless the information arrives in sequence, the pattern cannot function effectively. The wrong pattern may be selected as a result of information arriving out of sequence.
- *They demand continuity:* The natural tendency is to continue with the pattern, even when the problem has already been solved by applying only part of the pattern. The pattern system ensures that things will remain as they have been in the past.

The only way to get out of the predictable thinking process caused by the patterns is to challenge them.

## Challenging patterns

A dominant pattern suppresses all other patterns. Escaping from the dominant pattern means that the alternative solutions become possible and old ideas give way to new ones. The pattern system often means that the idea was there all the time but was unavailable because the dominant pattern hid it from view.

### *Changing the entry point*

Entering a pattern from a new point means that the path of the pattern may be forced to alter; it may become possible to see alternative patterns that have been hidden in the past. The dominant flow of the pattern may be such that the conventional entry point of the pattern always produces the same solution. Entering the pattern from a new point means that the flow of the pattern may be changed and the end may appear in a totally different place. This simply means starting from a point other than the one naturally chosen. You will need to force yourself to do this, sometimes by physically changing the position in which you do your thinking.

### *Starting at the end*

Starting with the solution and working back to the start of the problem makes the thinker see the problem from a new angle. This system is particularly useful when dealing with practical problems, such as making things fit into spaces or using set resources to produce an end product.

*Using discontinuity*

Jumping about within a pattern, refusing to follow the normal flow, causes the thinker to stop and re-examine the pattern from every angle. The points jumped to may have nothing to do with the pattern at all, but they can force a re-examination of a conventional pattern. The jump is unjustifiable before it is made, but since it may result in a new approach to an old problem, once made it can be justified. To do this requires a great deal of self-discipline. Having little cards, which you place in front of you and which introduce new ideas, will help. Once again, moving the thinking spot may be a solution too.

## Creative thinking techniques

Creative thinking involves two basic processes: escape and provocation.

To escape, you must:

- recognise dominant polarising ideas;
- deliberately search for alternative ways of looking at or doing things;
- refuse to accept any assumptions or to take anything for granted;
- ignore all existing concepts;
- attack your own and others' arrogance;
- realise that there are other ways of looking at things, which are concealed beneath the current way of looking at things;
- recognise the need to enlarge the problem concept and place attention on other areas;
- recognise the danger of the thought process being blocked by adequate ideas, which prevent the development of better ideas.

To be provocative, you will need to:

- separate the generation of ideas from the judgement and evaluation of those ideas;
- consider an idea to see where it can lead and what other ideas it can trigger off, rather than to see if it is correct;
- make unjustified leaps and then catch up with them;
- be wrong at some stages of the process in order to be right at the end;

- accept the fact that there may be no reason to say something until it is said - justify change only after change has occurred;
- use hindsight to justify an idea;
- use chance to create discontinuity.
- move for the sake of movement - create a direction, don't follow one.

To think creatively, you will need to develop an attitude of awareness, learn some simple techniques and skills, and learn to ignore the yes/no concept.

**Attitude of awareness**

Awareness is about realising the danger of being trapped by a fixed way of looking at things and of accepting the confines of an existing concept. It is about realising that there are two stages to the thinking process, logic and creativity, and that the two have different uses. Awareness will ensure that adequacy does not prevent the introduction of a better idea.

Awareness can't stop there; you need to recognise the dangers of arrogance and righteousness about a particular idea, and the need to use ideas in a practical manner and yet be willing to change them.

**Techniques and skills**

The techniques and skills of creative thinking can be learned even if the thinker does not accept the principles on which they are based. Techniques are merely the formal setting that encourage the use of creative thinking. Skill in creative thinking, like any other skill, comes with the practise of techniques.

Even if the techniques, once explained, are never used, an awareness of the principles involved can help the thinker to see the dangers of fixed ideas and the need to develop new ones.

The techniques employed, once the right attitude of awareness is engendered, are:

- recognition and categorisation of current ideas,
- changing ideas by avoidance,
- changing ideas from within,
- changing ideas from without,
- negation of the concept of judgement and evaluation.

*Recognition and categorisation of current ideas*

Current ideas are likely to fall into the following categories:

*Dominant:* Dominant ideas organise the approach to a problem in the same way that a dominant person organises a group. Sometimes the idea is specifically stated, and normally there is only a general awareness of it. Sometimes the idea is inherited with the situation; it may not even refer to the problem situation itself but rather to the way that the situation is looked at.

Having a vague notion of the dominant idea is not enough; it should be analysed and written down. At the start of any creative thinking process, the dominant ideas should be listed and thus put to one side. Removal of the idea(s) that dominates the thought processes helps to ensure that those processes can operate to the full.

*Crucial factors:* The dominant idea is large and overpowering whereas the crucial factor is small and insignificant, but unless it too is established, noted and subsequently ignored, creative thinking will be inhibited. Crucial factors are usually taken for granted; no one voices them in the open so they are very difficult to establish and note.

*Polarising tendencies:* Polarising tendencies are the either/or situations. They need to be discovered, noted and removed from the mind. The existence of such tendencies makes it impossible to hold an intermediate opinion. Creative thinking requires the holding of a complete range of opinions throughout the thought process.

*Boundaries:* Boundaries are limitations on the thought process: the limits beyond which the thinker cannot go. They must be recognised and removed from the thought process; creative thinking requires complete freedom to think.

*Assumptions:* Assumptions are needed to start the thinking process. They are the material that is fed in to help ideas grow. Some assumptions are valid, some invalid; that is not important in creative thinking. The mere existence of the assumption should be noted for fear that it may develop into a boundary or crucial factor.

Recognition of current ideas involves being aware of the limitations and restrictions and listing them so that they can be deliberately avoided.

*Changing ideas by avoidance*

This technique simply means stopping the thought process and directing it another way to see if new ideas can be generated. One idea, even one conceived by a creative thinker, can become dominant; thus to retain the ability to find other ideas, this must be prevented.

The methods employed are as follow:

- Note the idea and forget about it for a while. In a group session, use the phrase 'Let's leave that on a hook for a while.'
- Ask the question 'Why?', not as a justifying question, but rather as a method of opening up an idea for further examination.
- Deliberately consider different aspects of the problem, ignoring the core until all other aspects have been considered. Rotating a problem like this can bring out the areas that might have been taken for granted as being OK, but which are quite possibly the deep set roots of the problem itself.
- Think backwards. Instead of looking at the problem as a problem in search of a solution, consider a solution in search of a problem. List all the possible entry points to the problem, go through them all and pick out the most promising ones.
- Set a target for the number of solutions to be found and find them. Some of them will be very strange. No matter, your brain is now so desperate to collect ideas that it will forget to make judgements.
- Identify the major factors that relate to the problem. They may be brand names or certain fixed standards. Ignore them, now you are free to think.
- Instead of accepting a problem as a whole, break it down into key component parts, breaking those parts down even further until the full detail can be seen. Now think about all you see, not just the problem as first conceived.
- Bring contrasting thoughts together. Putting things together that have always been considered separately helps them to be seen in a totally different light.

*Changing ideas from within*

The approach of this technique is to take the ideas that exist and the current way of examining the situation and turn that around. The manner has to be unreasonable. If it were reasonable, it would merely be a logical development of the current situation.

The ways in which this can be achieved are as follows:

*Reversal:* The situation should be looked at in the opposite way to convention. Reversal is simply a technique for awakening new ideas; it does not matter how ridiculous the reversed situation may be.

*Distortion and exaggeration:* Over-emphasise a point to the ridiculous; distort the situation so that it seems entirely different. Once again, the more ridiculous the result, the more effective it may be in stimulating other thoughts.

*Changing ideas from without*

Change from without is the change that involves exposure, exposure to new and different circumstances and ideals. To ensure that exposure causes new thinking, it must be deliberately introduced. Change from without also involves the cross-fertilisation of ideas and problem switching; it involves the deliberate introduction of discontinuity.

*Exposure:* Exposure means relating the problem to other circumstances and things. It must be deliberate and random. The nature of the exposure is irrelevant. In using this technique, there must be a willingness to find significances and relationships. New ideas may be triggered at once by the exposure, or the experience of a new set of circumstances may help to generate future ideas.

*Cross-fertilisation:* The random element of cross-fertilisation is provided by people rather than things, as in exposure. Cross-fertilisation may mean setting up a brainstorming session; it may mean listening to people in different fields, talking about their problems; or it may mean tackling a problem in a field outside the thinker's own. The method simply generates new ideas from the influence of new experiences.

*Problem switching:* Problem switching means changing from one problem to another before the first problem has been solved. It can be particularly useful if someone has been tackling a problem for a long time. In a problem-solving situation, it may be worth-while setting up two problems to be solved at once, so that each problem may be assisted by the consideration of the other.

*Discontinuity:* The deliberate introduction of discontinuity is simply to help the thinker recharge the thinking processes and come up with new ideas. Two methods are useful: analogies and random words:

- *Analogies:* An analogy is described and the problem solver concentrates on the analogy, from time to time changing back to the original problem to see if the analogy has produced a new answer. This is the use of analogy to generate ideas, to get the problem moving. It is not argument by the use of analogy. The more incongruous the analogy, the more help it is likely to give in the creative thinking process.
- *Random words:* Completely irrelevant and totally random words are thrown into the thought process. The stimulus thus comes totally from outside and the word is totally irrelevant. A dictionary is the most convenient source of random words, but any other method can be used. The idea is to introduce complete discontinuity into the thought process to encourage the consideration of new ideas. To be totally random, the first word chosen must be used - it is wiser to take a noun than any other word form. The aim is to link the random word with the problem. The link may be a pun, the line of a song or simply a connected thought with the new word. Not too much time should be spend with such words; the purpose is simply to help stimulate thought in new areas.

*Negation of the concept of judgement and evaluation*

Logical thinking relies on judgement and evaluation; they play no part in creative thinking. An idea is an idea; it does not matter if it is good, bad or plain stupid; that idea may generate others. No evaluation can ever take place during creative thinking. No idea is rejected; it is merely listed and used to pass on to the next idea. Creative thinking may not be right at each step; indeed, to be wrong at least part of the time will help the thought process. The use of the word 'No' is best avoided in creative thinking exercises. It is too closely linked with the concepts of judgement and evaluation. The restriction of no longer using 'No' may cause the thought process to take a longer time than might otherwise be the case; but it will ensure that the restrictions of logical thinking are avoided.

Here are some ways of avoiding judgement and evaluation;

- *Be provocative:* Being provocative will help to avoid the negative. Try using the word 'Why?' the way that small children do.
- *Find something in between yes and no:* Try to accept that there is at present no yes or no answer to the situation under

consideration. In a group, the use of a word to stand for this meaning, such as 'Whoa', is simply a form of shorthand; a veto of any decision. In a solo thinking exercise, the use of the word can stop the thinker from using 'No'.

- *Collect unlikely words together:* Collect words that have no link beyond the fact that they have been linked for the moment; it is especially helpful to collect the opposing words. This provides another way of looking at different things together to see if they cause new ideas to be born. Sheets of paper can be used to carry lists of ideas which then must be considered together, the concept here being one of abnormality and change.
- *Change:* Change your ideas just as though someone has blown a whistle and demanded that everyone change their positions.
- *Pause:* Silence is a good way of stopping any judgements. If the thought is going too fast or too glibly, you will need time to think again.

## Brain maps

Brain maps are a method of taking notes that allows room for adaptation and change of thought. They allow you to record your creative thinking without being distracted by logical thought processes.

### How to brain map

A brain map can be produced in the following way (see the figure on page 67):

- Take a sheet of plain paper.
- Write the main idea or theme in the centre of the page.
- Draw a circle around the idea or theme.
- Attach related ideas to the theme with lines radiating from the centre word.
- Create sub-branches for each thought, related in turn to the branch lines.
- Use key words only to record the ideas.
- Review the completed pattern and consider the thoughts over again.
- Add to or eliminate the thoughts as they occur or are spoken.
- Emphasise key areas or linked areas with the use of colour coding.

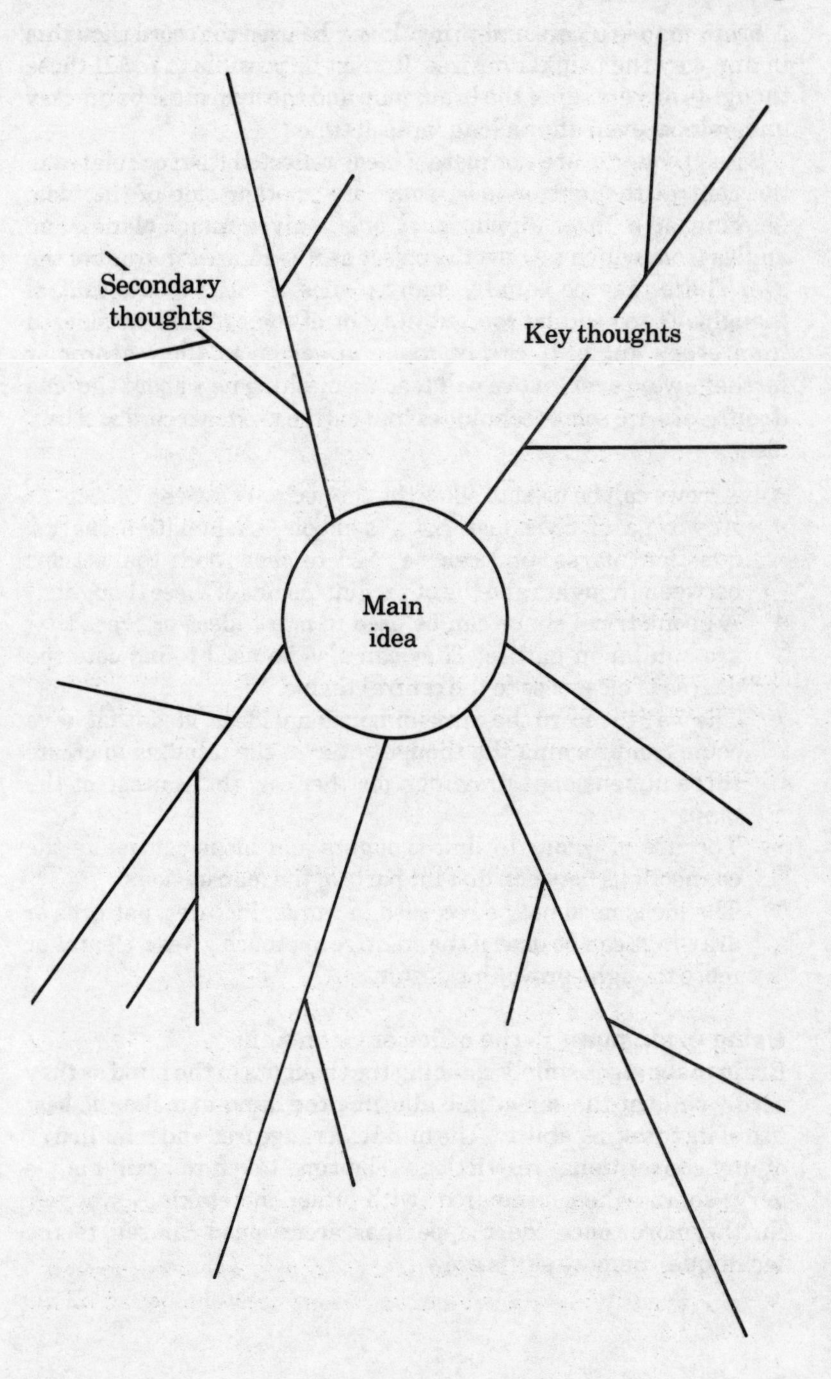
Secondary
thoughts
Key thoughts
Main
idea

A brain map is a personal thing. It can be used to record thoughts in any way the thinker desires. It must be possible to recall those thoughts on rereading the brain map and the map must be quickly understood, even after a long lapse of time.

Some thoughts are not merely ideas reflected from or related to the central thought or idea, some are another side of the idea. Looking at a three-dimensional object gives many planes and angles from which to view the object as it is rotated in front of the eye. There may be equally many planes of ideas to the central thought. It too can be rotated in front of the eye and considered from every angle. It can be made larger or smaller, nearer or further away; every move will teach something new about the idea itself. Here are some techniques that can be used to record and link ideas:

- Arrows can be used to show the connection between concepts.
- Any type of code (asterisks, symbols, exclamation marks, question marks, etc) can be used to show both connections between thoughts and the other dimensions of these thoughts.
- A geometrical shape can be used to mark ideas or areas that are similar in nature. They can also be used to indicate the degree of closeness to the central theme.
- The way to record the three-dimensional ideas, ideas that have come from turning the thought over in the mind, is to create three-dimensional drawings for them in the context of the map.
- The use of colour to link thoughts and ideas can make the connections between distant parts of the map obvious.
- The ideas need not be recorded in words. Pictures, patterns or drawings can be used if the creative approach gives a clearer or more thought-provoking result.

**Using brain maps in the office environment**

Brain mapping is simply catching the thoughts in the mind as they occur while at the same time allowing the mind to make the best use of its thinking ability. The mind can range free and remain free of any conventional restrictions. The time taken to brain map is very short when compared with other notetaking systems. Furthermore, once the mapper has accustomed himself to the technique, memory skills grow.

*Creating*
Using the brain map for any creative activity such as:

- writing a speech or lecture
- writing a report
- developing ideas

means that the thinking can range over the entire area to be thought about at all times during the creative activity. Once the map is completed, the information needed to accomplish the task is collected in one place in note form. The next stage is to emphasise the links, possibly using colour, and build any illustrative material on the bones of the piece. Symbols placed alongside some of the branches will indicate where the illustrative material should be and then the creator is ready to put the notes together in the required format.

*Note taking*
Taking notes for, say:

- lectures
- telephone conversations
- business deals
- meetings

means rapidly recording what has been said while still listening to the next stage of the conversation. The quicker the shorthand, the better; there is no time to stop and consider whether the notes are neat and verbatim. The brain mapper will start with a central theme and create a new branch each time a new element of the topic is introduced. Colour and symbols are particularly useful if the speaker or the meeting tends to wander from topic to topic; that way the linking themes can be emphasised and the notes will be more effective later.

If the notes of the meeting are intended for the notetaker's use only, they are best left as brain maps; if they are intended for the use of others or have to be written up as the minutes of the meeting, the mapper should use them in the same way as the speech writer.

*Planning*
Effective planning, whether for:

- personal matters
- meetings
- business

relies on thorough thinking and examination of the proposals; no restrictions should be placed on the process. The mapper can leave the planning map lying by his desk for days on end and return to it from time to time to add or alter ideas and thoughts. Kept by the side of the phone like a doodle, it becomes possible to make use of even very short periods of time in which to extend the planning process.

## Using creative skills in your organisation

Creativity may have been considered in the past to be the work of the marketing man or the research and development department only; that is not so. Every department in an organisation needs new ideas; every sphere benefits from the greater depth of thought that creative thinking brings to problems. It can be useful in the following situations:

*Decision making:* Creative thinking is open ended and thus might be thought to be out of place in a decision-making process. Its uses are:

- Setting goals and objectives, since they need to be as effective and well thought out as possible.
- Generating courses of action, from which to select the best or most appropriate course of action.
- Inserting pauses, which help the thinker think anew.

*Problem solving:* Problem solving is the recognition of a change situation. Something has to be done or changed to make the situation better. There is a need for change. Change too is the statement of a problem; the desire for change, once analysed, may identify a problem that is causing the longing for change.

Creative thinking is the thinking technique of change:

- Before making any attempt to tackle the problem, creative thinking can be used to make a list of possible approaches to the problem.
- When a problem has proved impossible to solve with ordinary logical thinking methods, the use of creative thinking helps to produce new angles on the problem.
- When a solution has been found that seems not quite perfect, creative thinking helps to find alternatives.

*Routine thinking:* Everyone needs to think for at least part of the day. No task can be done effectively without thought. Otherwise a robot could handle all the jobs in the world. Anyone who accepts the need to think should also consider the need to think creatively.

*Specific applications:* Creative thinking will automatically be more effective than logical thinking on the following occasions:

- where direct innovation is needed;
- simplification of an existing idea;
- regular periodic assessment of ideas to ensure that they still satisfy the need they were evolved to meet;
- problem solving;
- where change has occurred;
- where new information is produced;
- where there is a need to look at information in different ways;
- where a creative response is required;
- where there is a need to prevent the polarisation of ideas.

*Motivational force:* Motivated staff means an effective and happy organisation. Creative thinking is a good motivation-based technique, particularly when used in brainstorming sessions. Creative thinking involves the thinker in his or her environment and its problems; it offers a greater chance of solution of those problems, a higher chance of evaluation and puts all problems into context.

*Chapter 7*

# Decision Making

## The five-point, decision-making plan

To take an effective decision is simple, provided your thoughts and approach are organised. The five-point decision plan is designed to help you organise your thoughts. All decisions of any type can be effectively dealt with in this manner:

1. *Define the objective:* Specify the aim or objective, having recognised the need for a decision.
2. *Collect the information:* Collect and organise data, checking facts and opinions, identifying possible causes, and establishing time constraints and other criteria.
3. *Develop the opinions:* List possible courses of action and generate ideas.
4. *Evaluate and decide:* List the pros and cons, examine the consequences, measure against criteria, trial, test again the original objective and select the best.
5. *Implement:* Act to carry out the decision, monitor the decision and review.

## Define the objective

An effective decision is the best decision you are capable of making in the circumstances. You can't make that decision unless you know why it is being taken.

In the majority of decision-making situations, there is more than one possible solution, none of which can be perfect, because of the very nature of change and its influence on the decision process. The most accurate measure of an effective decision is at the time of its final outcome, possibly years away from the date the decision was made. Thus, the only way to evaluate a decision at the time of taking it is to apply a decision tree based on the balance between the four criteria:

- *aim* - achievement of aim;
- *cost* of implementation;
- *time* taken to implement;
- *acceptability* of the decision

To build a decision tree, you must examine the potential outcomes of each of the four criteria and reduce them to questions to be set at each stage of the decision. As soon as you reach an unacceptable answer, that decision must be reconsidered. Eventually, you will build up a picture of the perfect decision in the circumstances; however, if time was the major criterion, as in 'Was the building on fire?' you will have failed.

## Know your mind

In making your decision, you will use your brain, and so it would be helpful to understand how it works.

The brain contains approximately 10,000 million nerve cells. Each cell is capable of linking up with 10,000 of its neighbouring cells, which gives an infinitesimal figure of possible combinations. Something between 100,000 and 1,000,000 cells work when you need to make a decision. To use the power of your brain to make a decision that is both good and satisfying, you need to use three of the specific abilities of the brain:

- *Analysing* - the analysing section of the mind breaks down the whole into small digestible chunks, the complex into simple elements.
- *Synthesising or holistic thinking* - the synthesising section of the mind works in reverse to the analysing section; it enables you to tell the wood from the trees.
- *Valuing* - this is the judgemental, critical section of the mind that relies on brain patterns established by experience and learning to evaluate the decision being made.

If a decision is to be really effective, you must use all three abilities, and not just the one you enjoy the most.

The next problem in decision making is to deal with your depth mind. This is the part of the mind that issues sudden flashes of inspiration and intuition; it also has a key role in memory. It is the ability to think intuitively, which function relies on past, and particularly childhood, experience. The major problem in relying too heavily on the depth mind is the effect of your memory. Bad experiences teach a certain pattern of behaviour, which may rule out the logic of decision making. From the depth mind come:

- *Intuition* - the sure knowledge of a potential outcome with no logical justification for that knowledge.
- *Instinct* - the automatic reaction to a situation, even when the events are apparently occurring for the first time.
- *Emotion* - the reaction that has no base in logic, appears to fly in the face of value judgement and yet takes over.
- *Roadblocks* - the subconscious that controls fear of the unexplained and will not permit the open mind to change or learn.

## Analysing

Analytical ability establishes the relations of the parts to each other and to the whole, finds the true cause(s) of problems, identifies the issues at stake, discovers a law in nature and searches for the principles that lie behind experience. It involves:

- stripping the problem down to its bare essentials, as the solution may be buried under all the non-essential parts;
- looking regularly and in a consistent manner at the field in which you work so that you will be ready for the decisions that arise.

The analytical technique to decision making requires the skill of asking yourself questions. Not comfortable, rhetorical questions to emphasise the point in your mind, but effective, demanding questions that require a real answer. These questions should strip the decision of all pretensions and pare it down to the real criteria. To get to such a state you need to be puzzled:

> 'I keep six honest serving-men
> (They taught me all I knew);
> Their names are What and Why and When
> And How and Where and Who.'

*The analytical methods of logicians*
The logician is especially concerned with what can be properly concluded from statements or propositions. A set of two or more propositions and a conclusion are collectively called a 'syllogism':

> All coins are round *(major premise)*.
> You have a coin in your pocket *(minor premise)*.
> Your coin is round *(conclusion)*.

Logical thinking is the sense of being able to draw proper conclusions from information or evidence. The relationship between the premise and the conclusion is called 'inference'.

An advantage of disciplining the mind to logical thinking is that you become aware of the major part that premises play in decision making. If, however, your premises are generalisations, you will become aware of the need to clear your mind of such premises. For example, in the foregoing syllogism, the major premise is a generalisation, and a false one: all coins are not round. Thus, the conclusion fails too. The danger of generalisations and assumptions is clear; they lead to false conclusions and wrong decisions.

*How logicians analyse arguments*

In the foregoing syllogism, the reasoning might have gone:

| | |
|---|---|
| If *A*, then *B* | All coins *(A)* are round *(B)*. |
| *B* | You have a round object *(B)* in your pocket. |
| Therefore *A* | The object is a coin *(A)*. |

Logical reasoning centres on what may or may not be properly inferred. Algebra and mathematics are essentially logical because they rely on one piece of information to lead to the next.

*Inference in logic*

There are two key ways of inferring things: deductive and inductive. Deduction means drawing a particular inference from a general proposition, as illustrated by the following:

All shareholders are entitled to vote at the AGM.
All the directors are shareholders.
Therefore all the directors are entitled to vote at the AGM.

or according to Lewis Carroll, who produced some wonderful examples of logic:

No one takes *The Times* unless he is well educated.
No hedgehogs can read.
Those who cannot read are not well educated.
Therefore no hedgehog takes *The Times*.

Induction, on the other hand, is the inference of a generalisation from the consideration of a number of particular inferences, as in:

Product *A* sells very well in the North West test marketing area.
Product *A* will sell very well throughout the country.

In summary, to use analysis to help make a decision:

- analyse the factors in depth;
- analyse the general situation;
- apply logic;
- think backwards, if the desired end is there;
- organise the facts;
- look for the logic in the situation.

## Synthesising or holistic thinking

Holistic thinking is the opposite to analysis. This type of thinking views the problem as a whole, rather than breaking it down into small parts.

In business, there is often the danger that each department sees a decision-making problem in the light of the way it affects them. It becomes a 'production decision', a 'sales problem', an 'accounts matter', etc. Viewed as a whole, it has the priorities of the entire organisation to contend with. To think and decide holistically, you need to know and support the objectives of the organisation. Why is it here? And what are you doing to help it achieve its objectives? Thinking in concepts is the way to work with holistic thinking. All concepts are abstract. Holistic concepts are not the same as abstract analysis; on the contrary, the concept is itself a developing situation.

While the word 'concept' cannot be effectively defined, it can be illustrated by examples:

- communication
- finance
- motivation
- wealth
- participation

all being concepts that apply in any organisation. To make a decision without considering the elements of the decision from those conceptual points of view will negate the effectiveness of the decision made.

The most important concept to take into consideration while trying to make a management decision is the concept of the whole organisation, which really means that, alongside the financial models, you need to build conceptual ones.

## Valuing

Decision making rests on establishing the truth and knowing what to do. The risk is that too many decision makers skimp the first, relying on the more action-orientated second to carry them through.

Despite being the most subjective and personal element of the decision-making trio of talents, valuing is the only way to establish the truth. It relies on your understanding of values as they exist, and as they apply to the three characteristics of the decision, the organisation and yourself.

The only way to make effective value judgements, and thus lead to effective decisions, is to set a code of values by which you and anyone in the organisation will judge. To do this, you must:

- establish any inherent assumptions and prejudices that may mar your value judgement;
- acknowledge their existence and learn to avoid them;
- establish any code of value required of or by the organisation such as
  - company law
  - employment law
  - social behaviour patterns accepted in the country of trade
  - company procedures, laid down and implied;
- review regularly any codes of values discovered;
- establish any particular value criteria applicable to the decision.

To set your criteria either generally or for particular decision-making circumstances, you may need to consult specialists. By definition, the role of the top manager or leader in any organisation is that of a specialist. His specialism is to run and control the organisation: as such he should not be expected to control detail within every section of that organisation. Thus, it follows that he needs to consult down the line in order to make such judgements.

## Collect the information

If you employ the full decision-making talents of your mind, you will need to collect all the facts from all the people who are likely to know and be involved. To do so, you must retain the full use of your open mind. It is too easy to be swayed by the first facts you meet and to half-make the decision, and then to bend any other facts until they fit the predisposed plan.

**How to keep an open mind**

Take a sheet of paper and divide it up as shown in the following example. Use it to collect all your thoughts and take it with you when you go to find the facts. Read it regularly.

**Open mind sheet**

*Subject*

___

___

*Dominant thoughts*

How the organisation sees the problem at the moment. How you see the problem at the moment.

___

___

___

___

___

___

*Crucial factors*

The small insignificant details that stop you taking the big decisions.

___

___

___

___

___

___

*Polarising tendencies*

The either/or situations.

___

___

___

___

___

___

*Boundaries*
The limits beyond which you think you cannot go.

*Assumptions*
All your assumptions on the subject, however shaming they are.

## Develop the options

Having sorted out the objectives and established the facts, you will still not be able to make a totally effective decision because you will not have examined all the options The art of developing or extending the options just far enough, and not too far, is the real art of effective decision making. One problem with extending the options too far is that so many options may present themselves that it may seem even harder to make the final decision. Another is that it becomes easier to procrastinate while pleading that the time is to be spent looking for further options. Nevertheless, it is essential, in taking an effective decision, to ensure that all reasonably possible options have been examined.

**Developing a range of options**
You are not seeking all the possibilities of action, merely a sufficient range to ensure that the best decision can be taken. This can be done in the following ways:

- *Do nothing:* Never forget that the do-nothing option always exists. It may, of course, not be worth consideration, but it certainly should not be forgotten.
- *History:* Look at past options to see if similar circumstances apply, and consequently whether the same options could still be viable.
- *Brainstorming:* Get a group together and try out ideas to see if new options emerge (see Chapter 6).
- *Creative thinking:* The one-person brainstorming session that seeks the unusual or oddball idea (see Chapter 6).
- *Analogy:* Analogy is the technique of comparing two situations that apparently have nothing in common. Consider a business decision and relate it to a child's fairy story or to a domestic problem. Examine the business decision using the characters and events from the story or domestic event to people the stage.
- *Idea banks:* Set up idea banks, filing cabinet drawers full of thought-provoking papers or information. Share idea banks on general subjects and use them to trigger specific ideas.

## Imaginative thinking

Imaginative thinking is a way of thinking in pictures. All minds have a fundamental visual capacity, although some people are able to use this capacity better than others.

Thinking in pictures uses five clear techniques:

- *Recall* - the ability to bring back to mind something that happened in the past.
- *Visualising* - the ability to form a picture of something not experienced in its entirety.
- *Creating* - the ability to form the image of something that does not exist at all at present.
- *Foreseeing* - the ability to see a development or outcome before it happens. Second sight?
- *Fantasy* - the ability to invent novel and unreal happenings by altering or combining the elements of reality in a particularly unrestrained manner.

In expanding the options to make a decision, recall, visualising and creating have a real contribution to make. Foreseeing also has a contribution to make, provided that it is true foreseeing and not a case of outright pessimism or optimism unbacked by a real ability.

*Imagination in perspective*
Imagination is not the most effective option-finding technique. it is one of the techniques that may be chosen. Decision making, and in particular option seeking, should not be seen as a golden opportunity to let facts fly to the wind.

Change does mean innovation and development, however, and progress requires these two elements; thus, there is plenty of room for imagination in every career.

**How imaginative are you?**
If you have a good imagination you will be better able to expand the options. To establish the level of your imagination, tick the boxes in response to the following questions:

☐ 1. Can you recall visually with great accuracy? (Imagine your last business meeting and determine how much detail you can see in the mental pictures.)

☐ 2. Can you recall in colour?

☐ 3. Would you describe yourself as good at visualising things which you have not yourself experienced directly?
(Imagine what it would be like to be a member of your staff.)
(Imagine what it would be like to live abroad.)

☐ 4. Can you create a picture in your mind in response to a phrase or word?
(Wine lake; big bang.)

☐ 5. Has anyone commended you for your imagination within the last year?

☐ 6. Have you invented or made anything recently?

☐ 7. Do you tend to foresee accurately what happens before the event?

☐ 8. Do you fantasise about your work or career?

☐ 9. Do you paint or draw?

☐ 10. Do you find it easy to choose colour schemes?

☐ 11. Do you find that you can think up names for pets and children?

☐ 12. Have you ever written a story or poem?

☐ 13. Have you ever composed a piece of music?

☐ 14. Could you create a sentence using only pictures?

## Evaluate and decide

### Decision-making style

The decision maker in an organisation will need to employ one or other of the following styles:

*Autocratic*

The group leader solves the problem, using the information he possesses. He does not consult with anyone else nor seek information in any form. This style assumes that the leader has sufficient information to examine all the relevant options and make an effective decision, but that is rarely the case.

*Information seeking*

When the leader does not possess sufficient information to make an effective decision, he will need to obtain information or skill from others. He may not tell them what the problem is; normally, he simply asks for information. The leader then evaluates the information and makes the decision.

*Consultation*

The leader explains the situation to the group or individual whom he provides with relevant information, and together they generate and evaluate solutions. Alternatively, he may ask the group or individual to conduct a survey/investigation and make recommendations. Finally, the leader evaluates the solutions or recommendations the group or individual has put forward and then makes a decision, which may or may not take these views into account.

*Negotiation*
The leader explains the situation to the group or individual and provides the relevant information. Together they attempt to reconcile differences and negotiate a solution that is acceptable to all parties. The leader may consult with others before the meeting in order to prepare his case and generate alternative decisions that are acceptable to him.

*Delegation*
Responsibility and authority for making the decision are given to the group or individual. The leader provides all the relevant information that he possesses. The leader's role then becomes that of chairman. He guides and controls the discussion but does not attempt to force his opinions on the group. He is prepared to accept and implement any solution proposed by the group or individual.

## Decision making in meetings

Part of the thrust of decision making is thinking style. Argument, the mainstream of group discussion, often forms part of the decision-making process. Rational argument, a free and open encounter in search of the truth, implies some rules, some common acceptance of criteria and a common commitment to the truth sought. The win-at-all-costs mentality will lead to loss at some stage, and to deception and tricks to ensure that the loser is not self-selected. It is, however, difficult to steer away from such an approach, especially when the decision needs to be taken in a competitive environment.

The following are the techniques *not* to apply in group decision making, or the exercise of rational argument:

- *Playing the individual and not the ball*
  - Trying to use decisions to score over an individual.
  - Trying to use emotive pressures such as money or status to persuade.
  - Appealing to envy or prejudice.
  - An argument directed at ignorance from superior knowledge.
- *Argument by analogy*
  - The value of analogy is in inventing more options.
  - The danger of analogy is in extending false analogies and assuming that the decision is made because the solution applies in the analogy.

- *Rationalising*
  - — Rationalisation is the asking for reasons where reasons should not apply.
  - — The risk of using rationalisation to justify negative attitudes is high.
  - — Rationalising can also be a form of buck passing, the invention of scapegoats of one type or another.
- *Drawing irrelevant conclusions*
  - — The *non sequitur* of one line of reasoning to another.
  - — Red herrings and diversions come in all shapes and sizes, often when the argument is at its weakest.
- *Reduction to absurdity*
  - — A good way to destroy a thesis is to reduce it to the absurd.
  - — Since the absurd rarely occurs, the argument is self-destructive.
- *No decision/no action*
  - — A tempting solution often ushered in with the words 'Leave it till we're not so busy' or 'Let's set up a committee to decide this one'.
  - — Making no decision is indeed a clear and valid option, but it may not be the right option.
  - — Where it's a case of solution *A* as opposed to solution *B* or no action, and both *A* and *B* bring fewer problems than no action, a decision has to be made.
- *All and some*
  - — The abstraction of the infrequent or frequent occurrence to be accepted as the norm.
  - — Statistics often lead to all and some errors.
- *Middle of the road*
  - — The assumption that truth never lies in extremes is false.
  - — Just as is the assumption that there is a link between opposites.

All of the above are most likely to occur during group decision taking. If you think they have occurred or are likely to occur during your decision-making meetings, turn to Chapter 9.

**Simple decision-making techniques**

The simple decision making techniques apply to the vast majority of cases where a decision is to be taken. They are as follows:

- establish the possible options;
- sort out the feasible options;
- proceed by elimination;
- apply the criteria of
  - — aim
  - — cost
  - — time
  - — acceptability

  to eliminate each of the feasible options until two options remain;
- check that the alternatives are true alternatives, and not two sides of the same coin;
- establish whether both can be attempted or whether they are mutually exclusive;
- re-examine the objectives to establish whether one will compromise them;
- consider the option of doing nothing;
- if the decision has still not emerged, toss a coin; in those circumstances, all things must be equal.

*Limitations affecting management choice*
The real limits will need to be established in each of the following areas:

- time
- information
- resources
- knowledge

*Probability*
The probability of an event occurring must be considered. Risk is only worth taking if the likelihood of it achieving the sought after objective is probable.

*Developing your skills*
In Lord Thompson's autobiography *After I was Sixty;* he gave this advice:
- The way to become good at decision making is to take lots of decisions in your field.
- See relationships between your decisions, despite differences of time, place and scale.
- Look on your brain as a mental computer.

- Shun mental laziness
- Be willing to make the effort that good decision making requires.

Commonsense adds the following checklist to the development of decision-making skills:

- *Know yourself and your limitations*
  — Take on the things you can do.
  — Ask for help when you need it.
  — Review your skills regularly.
- *Learn on the job*
  — If you make a mistake, don't write it off, learn by it.
  — Don't issue blame, look for solutions.
- *Keep mentally fit*
  — Don't try to take decisions when you're tired.
  — Keep stress under control.
  — Use your brain; using it keeps it alive.
- *Keep your imagination alive*
  — Try new things.
  — Look for ideas.
  — Read newspapers and books.
  — Listen to the opinions of others.
  — Keep your mind open.
  — Seek out new experiences.
  — Keep your mental batteries charged.

## Implement

People do what you check up on. You will do what you check up on yourself. The best self-check is to tell others what you intend to do and then let them check up on you.

**Write a plan**

- Set out the main objectives of the job.
- When undertaking the task, compare your actual activities with the objectives listed.
- Note any past problems or difficulties.
- Conclude how the job is to be tackled.

**Decide what can be delegated**

- List what cannot be delegated.
  - — tasks beyond the skills of others
  - — confidential and security matters
  - — disciplinary matters.
- List the routine tasks.
- List the time-consuming tasks.

**Decide who is to do the task**

- Who has time?
- Who is ready for new challenges?
- What training will be needed?

**Set the task in motion**

- Define the task in writing.
- Establish the problems and pitfalls of the task.
- Define any additional authority needed.
- Establish the authority.
- Explain the task, its pitfalls and its good points.
- Go through the task with those who are to undertake it.
- Set report-back targets for everyone involved.
- Monitor, which means standing back and watching, not taking over.

# *Chapter 8*
# Leadership

Leadership is one of the most difficult qualities to describe. It is perhaps the ability to get others to value your judgement sufficiently to enable them to decide to do as you ask. Anyone can be a good leader, but first they have to want to and, second, they have to adopt the right style or approach.

## The basic steps to being a good leader

- *Establish who is in charge*
  - People must trust you and accept you as an authority figure.
  - Gain credibility.
- *Know what you want to accomplish*
  - Define your own goals, and the organisation's.
  - Plan.
- *Know what you want each person in the team to accomplish*
  - Set realistic goals and targets.
  - Measure achievement.
- *Let people know what you expect*
  - Communicate with the group.
  - Never assume people know or don't want to know.
- *Find out what your employee wants for himself*
  - What motivates him, what needs does he have?
  - Listen to what he says.
- *Find out what your employee expects of you*
  - Listen.
  - Don't play Faerie Queen/King of the Castle.
- *Take being a role model seriously*
  - Never undermine authority.
  - Act as you require others to act.
- *Expect others to be self-motivated but don't count on it*
  - Part of your responsibility is to motivate others.

- *Understand that the quality of your leadership is determined by the methods you choose to motivate others*
  — Think before you react.

## Behaviour patterns of leaders

To lead effectively, you need to be able to behave in the following nine definite ways, all at the same time. Leading is a job for the calm and level headed who can care.

- *Initiation:* The leader initiates, facilitates or resists new ideas and practices.
- *Membership:* The leader mixes with the group, stresses informal interaction between himself and members or interchanges personal services with members.
- *Representatation:* The leader defends the group against attack, advances the interests of the group and acts on behalf of the group
- *Integration:* The leader subordinates individual behaviour, encourages a pleasant group atmosphere, reduces conflict between members and promotes individual adjustment to the group.
- *Organisation:* The leader defines or structures his own work, the work of other members and the relationships among members in the performance of their work.
- *Domination:* The leader restricts the behaviour of individuals or the group in action, makes decisions and expresses opinions.
- *Communication:* The leader provides information to members, seeks information from them, facilitates the exchange of information and shows awareness of any matter relating to the group.
- *Recognition:* The leader behaves in such a way that either expresses approval or disapproval of the behaviour of group members.
- *Production:* The leader sets levels of effort or achievement, or prods members for greater effort or achievement.

The ideal leader has the support of the members of his group in every dimension of his activity.

## Sources of influence

A leader can exert influence on his subordinates in several ways:

- *Coercive power:* This is based on fear. The fear can be physical or psychological. In business, this is usually the fear of being fired or of receiving an undesirable work assignment. Coercive power should be used sparingly and only as a last resort.
- *Reward power:* This is the opposite of coercive power. Co-operating with the leader means a positive reward, either monetary or psychological. Reward power is available to most managers. For it to be effective, however, there must be a direct and observable relationship between accomplishing group objectives and receiving the reward. It is not unusual for a group to try to negate reward power by punishing those workers who respond to it.
- *Legitimate power:* This is the type of power that emanates from superior status in the organisational framework; it closely resembles authority. Such power is effective if the group accepts the leader. If not reinforced by other sources of power, it is less influential.
- *Expert power:* This is the power residing in a person who has some special knowledge or expertise that has enabled him to gain the respect and co-operation of the group. Ideally a manager has enough expertise with a project to command this sort of power. If the manager has to turn to someone else for expertise, that other person will share some of the manager's power.
- *Referent power:* This is the power based on the subordinate's identification with the leader. Followers may not like the individual, but they respect the leader, and as a result they respect the leader's chosen one.

For managers, the following implications apply:

- The more numerous the sources of influence available to a leader, the greater the effectiveness he can manifest.
- Some sources of influence overlap. For example, reward and legitimate sources of influence often go hand in hand, whereas referent and expert sources are frequently related.
- Without influence, the leader will be usurped.

The art and practice of good leadership is choosing the right behaviour emphasis and mixing it with the right level of power on every occasion. Being infallibly right is not easy. What you need is help in choosing the right style of leadership for the people and the organisation and a checklist of what to do and when.

## Leadership styles

Leadership styles are influenced by many factors: at one end of the scale is the autocratic manager; at the other end is the democratic manager.

**Boss-centred leadership**
This type of leadership can be characterised as follows:

| | *Percentage of extension of authority of manager* | *Percentage of freedom for subordinate* |
|---|---|---|
| Manager makes decision and announces it | 100 | 0 |
| Manager sells decision | 80 | 20 |
| Manager presents ideas and invites questions | 60 | 40 |
| Manager presents tentative decision, subject to change | 50 | 50 |

**Subordinate-centred leadership**
This type of leadership is characterised by the following:

| | *Percentage of extension of authority of manager* | *Percentage of freedom for subordinate* |
|---|---|---|
| Manager presents problem, gets suggestions, makes decision | 40 | 60 |
| Manager defines limits, asks group to make decision | 20 | 80 |
| Manager permits subordinates to function within set limits | 0 | 100 |

There may be a place for each of these leadership positions on the management scale depending on the people involved and the task to be tackled, as follows:

100/0 per cent
The team is very junior, the task is to be performed once only, the team has come together for the occasion. Even in these circumstances, it is important to realise the potential effect on motivation and morale of such autocratic leadership. Perhaps its only real place is where the building is on fire and the manager takes the decision for evacuation.

80/20 per cent
Once again, the team is junior and probably very new. The task is crucial to the organisation and no alteration to company policy can be permitted. The act of selling the decision has the opportunity of ensuring that the manager takes every opportunity to maintain morale and motivation.

60/40 per cent
The team in question has clear objectives but can achieve success without high levels of interdependency. The team members have distinctive roles with individual responsibilities. Perhaps a group of experts are pooling advice in order to maximise achievement for the organisation. Morale and motivation are not the responsibility of the manager.

50/50 per cent
A group of experts in control of an organisation who need directive leadership. In other words, probably the ideal leadership style for a board of directors and the chairman. Also useful where the decision is not important to the organisation, but development of the learning curve of the group is very high priority.

40/60 per cent
Members of the group are fairly senior and experienced. Their roles are interdependent and they need to be effective and competent to perform. The team as a unit makes a significant contribution to organisational effectiveness. Demotivation would lead to poor performance, wasted opportunities and low morale.

20/80 per cent
Members of the team are highly independent and collectively responsible for achieving major objectives that have a significant effect on the organisation's profitability or effectiveness. Survival

of the organisation relies on the use of the skills of this effective team. Such leadership requires a strong and respected manager.

0/100 per cent
Delegation has taken place to a trained and efficient member of staff. This occurs every time a letter is dictated. The manager must, however, retain responsibility for the task being undertaken. As such, he must continue to monitor and to demonstrate his ultimate responsibility.

Whatever the style of leadership operative for the task in hand, the leader has three major responsibilities:

- to get that task accomplished;
- to build the morale of the team undertaking the task;
- to develop each of the individuals involved in the task.

Which is why by far the best system of leadership is that promoted by John Adair and described as action-centred leadership.

## Action-centred leadership

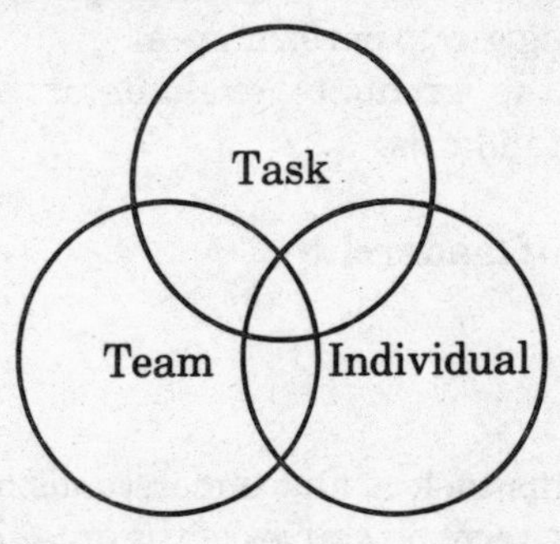


*Source:* John Adair, *The Action-Centred Leader* (Kogan Page)

When describing this style of leadership, the following activities must be considered:

- *Planning* - seeking all available information
  - Defining group task, purpose of goal.
  - Making a workable plan.
- *Initiating* - briefing group on the aims and the plan
  - Explaining why aim or plan is necessary.
  - Allocating tasks to group members.
  - Setting group standards.

- *Controlling* - maintaining group standards
  - — Influencing tempo.
  - — Ensuring all actions are taken towards objectives.
  - — Keeping discussion relevant.
  - — Prodding group to action or discussion.
- *Supporting* - expressing acceptance of persons and their contribution
  - — Encouraging group or individuals.
  - — Disciplining group or individuals.
  - — Creating team spirit.
  - — Relieving tension with humour.
  - — Reconciling disagreements or getting others to explore them.
- *Informing* - clarifying task and plan
  - — Keeping the group in the picture.
  - — Receiving information from the group.
  - — Summarising suggestions and ideas coherently.
- *Evaluating* - checking feasibility of an ideal
  - — Testing the consequences of a proposed solution.
  - — Evaluating group performance.
  - — Helping the group to evaluate its own performance against standards.

## Responsibilities of leadership

*Achieving the task*

The efficient leader:

- is clear what his task is and understands how it fits into the long- and short-term objectives of the organisation;
- plans how to accomplish it;
- defines and provides the resources needed;
- ensures that each member of the group has clearly defined targets for improving performance;
- plugs any gaps in the abilities of the group by training and development;
- constantly evaluates results and monitors progress towards goals.

*Keeping group morale high*
The leader:

- provides regular opportunities for briefing the group;
- provides regular opportunities for genuine consultation before reaching decisions affecting the group;
- accords the official representative of the group the facilities he needs to be its effective spokesman;
- ensures that there is a formal and fair grievance procedure understood by all.

*Getting the best out of each individual*
The leader will see that each person:

- gets a sense of personal achievement in his job;
- feels he is making a worthwhile contribution;
- is told if his performance is unsatisfactory and given help to improve;
- feels that his job challenges him and his capabilities are matched by the responsibilities given to him;
- receives adequate recognition for his achievements.

*Being the best leader*
Is someone who:

- is human, treating subordinates as human beings;
- does not bear a grudge, has no favourites, and is fair to the group as well as to the organisation;
- is easy to talk to and listens;
- is honest, keeps his word and doesn't dodge unpleasant issues;
- drives himself hard - others don't mind him expecting the best of them.

## How to build a team

- *Establish clear aims*
  — Intelligent groups can often find their own way if they know where to go.
  — People are often bogged down with methods.
- *Don't be over-ambitious at the start*
  — Success builds both confidence and further success.
  — People relax when they understand what they are doing.

- — Those who do understand feel good, the others learn quickly.
- — No one feels threatened.

- *Make sure everyone agrees before taking any action*
  - — Commitment comes from real understanding.
  - — Change without commitment is almost impossible.
  - — Gaining commitment is time consuming.
- *Build realistic timetables*
  - — Unlearning often needs to precede learning.
  - — Cultural changes come slowly.
  - — There is always something to go wrong.
- *Consult widely and listen to the replies*
  - — People do have valuable contributions to make.
  - — Consultation increases commitment.
  - — Manipulation undermines team building
- *Relate team building to organisational work*
  - — Experimentation is more likely to be accepted if it does not involve substantial extra work.
  - — Use regular meetings as team-building opportunities.
  - — Meaningful results are more easily identified.
- *Face up to the problems*
  - — Don't ignore the difficult.
  - — Be realistic about what is attainable.
  - — Playing politics will discredit your efforts.
- *Encourage openness and frankness*
  - — Deep-rooted prejudices and beliefs are more easily dealt with if discussed openly.
  - — Don't stifle discussion.
- *Don't raise false expectations*
  - — Promises are easy.
  - — Broken promises discredit.
- *Recognise work*
  - — Developmental activities take time.
  - — Team building can increase individual work-loads.
- *Remember the threat of the unknown*
  - — When problems are exposed they become less threatening.
- *Development is basically self-regulated*
  - — Age, capacity and beliefs can create limitations.
  - — Ultimately, you are responsible for your own development.

- *Force does not work*
  - — People cannot be forced into attitude changes.
  - — People cannot be forced into openness and honesty.
  - — People can be forced into pretending to change.
- *Remember those who are not part of the action*
  - — Jealousy can develop.
  - — People like to be involved.
- *Team building can precipitate other problems*
  - — Other groups can feel insecure.
  - — Individuals and teams can grow beyond their present roles.
- *Be open to other opportunities when team building*
  - — Individual development can occur.
  - — New ideas generate further creativity.
  - — Challenges to existing systems and methods may present themselves.
- *Delegate*
  - — People have different strengths and skills.
  - — Delegation usually means development.
- *Accept external help if necessary.*
  - — Choose carefully.
  - — Take responsibility for your own actions.
  - — Outsiders offer different insights and skills.
    Outsiders do not have organisational histories.
  - — Outsiders are more likely to be impartial.
- *Learn from mistakes*
  - — Admit it when you are wrong.
  - — Review progress regularly.
  - — Encourage feedback.
  - — Honest feedback is the most valuable thing your colleagues can give you.
- *Practise what you preach*
  - — Actions speak louder than words.

To ensure it works, the team must:

- reflect on its work methods and set targets for improvement;
- develop a self-discipline that uses time and resources well;
- be given sufficient opportunities to meet and work through any problems;
- support members;
- have open relationships and be prepared to confront difficulties.

## *Chapter 9*
# Meetings

## Making use of meetings

Since so many meetings seem to operate in a ratio of 10 units of time wasted to 1 unit of actual achievement, the rationale for holding a meeting is frequently in doubt. Before a meeting is held the following checklist needs to be answered:

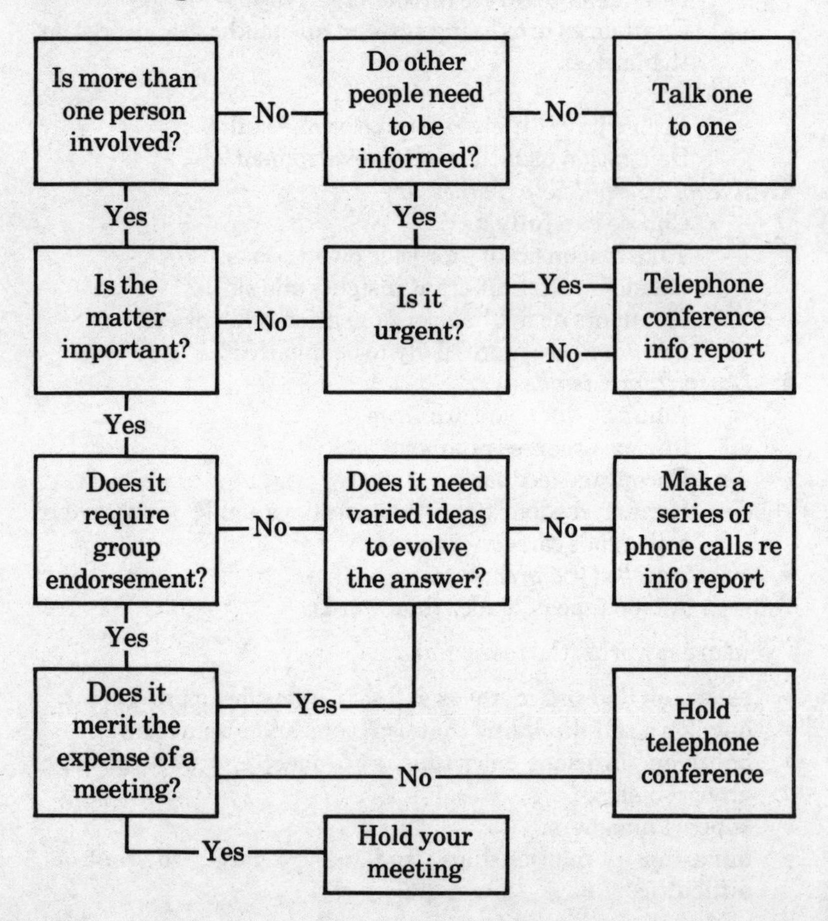

Also, you need to take into account the following additional decision-making criteria:

- If communication is to be successful, each person needs to read or hear the same facts. A meeting may save communication failures.
- A poor meeting is invariably worse than no meeting, because it demotivates; only good meetings motivate.
- Effective time managers plan their time with care. Only use meetings where they will be effective.

Most people hate meetings. If you ask them why, the answer they give you can be summed up as poor chairmanship. Meetings often fail to meet their achievement targets and as a result become time wasters because:

- the purpose is not stated clearly;
- wrong participants attend;
- too many meetings are held;
- poor or no minutes are published;
- irrelevant talk takes place;
- no conclusions are drawn at the meeting;
- no follow-up takes place;
- indecision means that the meeting achieves nothing;
- the meeting fails to start on time;
- too many interruptions occur during the meeting;
- the chairman does not stick to the agenda;
- the meeting goes on too long.

All of which is a shame, because good meetings can motivate everyone involved and make the task of getting things done far easier.

The simplest and most basic way in which a number of individuals become a team or group is by attending regular meetings. The meeting creates a sense of belonging and joint responsibility; it is a base for good leadership.

Meetings help groups to form effectively, set up the structure and rules under which they can best work, and breed loyalty.

Meetings help each member of the team to understand the collective aim of the group and the way in which his own work can contribute to the group's success. They put membership of a group into proportion.

Greater commitment to group decisions is obtained through involvement in the decision-making process. When a member argues against a decision in the group, the only alternative to accepting the majority vote is to leave the group altogether.

Group decisions often carry greater authority than individual decisions and as such become more acceptable to the organisation's hierarchy.

The management structure of organisations often means that the only time teams are physically gathered together is at meetings. It is often only at the meeting that the leader of a group can be perceived as such, rather than as a person doing a job.

A meeting is a status arena - a chance for each member to demonstrate his standing and worth within the organisation.

Use your meetings to make group ties stronger and to motivate members. Remember the demotivation factors of bad organisation and supervision and avoid the common meeting faults.

## Rules for meetings

There are two common problems linked with meetings: size and the frequency with which the meeting is to be held.

### Size

Meetings fall into roughly three size categories:

- *The assembly:* 100 or more people who are present to listen to the main speaker(s). They may contribute at question time.
- *The council:* 40 or 50 people who are there mainly to listen to appointed spokesmen but who can come forward with questions and comments and who may be asked to contribute something on their own account.
- *The committee:* up to 10, or at the most 12, people all of whom speak more or less on equal footing under the guidance and control of the chairman.

### Frequency

- *The daily meeting:* For those who work together on the same project to reach decisions of a uniform nature by informal general agreement.
- *The weekly or monthly meeting:* For those who work on different but parallel projects, where there is a certain

competitive element and a greater likelihood that the chairman will make the final decision himself.

- *The irregular or occasional meeting:* For people whose normal work does not bring them into contact and whose work has little or no relationship to the others'. They are united only by the project that the meeting exists to promote and motivated by the desire that the project should succeed.

Your problems are bound to lie in the second and third frequency committee meetings.

## Before the meeting

Effective meetings are the ones that have been properly planned. It takes time to think out the right way to tackle a meeting to make sure that:

- the right *objectives* are set;
- the right *people* meet;
- the *timing* is right;
- the *agenda* covers all the right things.

### Setting objectives

Just as every businessman and woman needs, from time to time, to answer the question 'Why am I here?', so every meeting needs to be considered from the same questioning standpoint, 'Why are we all here?' The best objective-setting questions are:

- What is this meeting intended to achieve?
- What would be the likely consequences of not holding the meeting?
- How can its failure or success be judged?

One thing is certain: if you don't clearly understand why you are calling the meeting, the other participants will be unsure too, and a great deal of time will be wasted.

Meetings can only achieve the following definite objectives:

*Information-digestive*

- The presentation of information from a particular person that also allows questions and feedback.
- Used for important items that require the support of the team.
- Includes progress reports to keep the group up to date on the current status of projects.

- Used where informing each individual member separately might confuse and where written handouts are not sufficient.

*Constructive-originative*
- The search for new ideas or policies.
- To encourage every member of the meeting to contribute knowledge, experience and judgement.

*Executive responsibilities*
- The 'how to put into action' meeting.
- Allocation of executive responsibilities for areas of a task.
- The allocation of such responsibilities could be done outside a meeting but the following make a meeting desirable:
  — the group can find the best way of achieving objectives;
  — each member can understand and influence the best way in which his own job will fit in with the overall objectives of the meeting;
  — forming your own action plan gets commitment;
  — volunteers will be forthcoming.

*Legislative framework*
- Keeping status intact.
- Essential in order to get commitment to any hierarchical changes made.
- Helping the organisation to grow and develop through change.

## People

Since people are the 'stuff' of meetings, they can be the most effective cause of their failure.

*Numbers*
If there are too many people, the meeting turns into a council. Each person will have at least one opinion, probably two.

*Rule:* Keep the numbers as low as possible: 4 to 7 is generally ideal; 12 is the outside limit.

*Who*
The right people need to attend. *Never* select people because they think they should come; they have always come; they want to sit in as observers; they are afraid of missing out.

*Rule:* Those who attend have a contribution to make; only relevant people attend.

To keep the numbers down consider:

- attendance for particular items only;
- holding two smaller meetings in place of one large;
- using working parties to bring reports to the full meeting.

People who plead they are very busy can be persuaded by their own statements to stay away from the meetings they are complaining about: let them eliminate themselves rather than offend sensitivities.

*Readiness*
Insist that all members read the agenda before the meeting and come prepared to speak on the topics listed.

*Rule:* Send out papers in good time; make the need to read and consider in advance clear; remove a subject from the agenda if insufficient preparation seems to have been done - you will only have to do it once.

## Timing

The right people, clear objectives and the wrong timing, and still the meeting can fail.

*Start*
Set a starting time and start then, even if you are the only person in the room.

*Finish*
State a finishing time on all the papers of the meeting and do not overrun.

*Day*
Think about the members when setting the day. You may not get full attention on Monday morning or Friday afternoon. Give enough time for the meeting to carry out its ideas.

*Time*
Owls will not be at their best in the morning; larks will fade in the afternoon. No one is at their best after a heavy lunch.

*Length*
People lose concentration after 45 minutes, so keep the subject matter in maximum 45-minute bands. People fail to take in as much information after 2 hours without a break, so if it is to be a long meeting build in breaks.

*Rule:* 2 hours is the maximum for one effective meeting; 3 hours is the very top limit (a break must be built in midway); 1½ hours is the right meeting length.

## Agenda

The agenda is vital to the meeting; without one, no control would be possible. A properly drawn up agenda has the power of both shortening and clarifying a meeting.

The purpose of the agenda is twofold:

- to answer 'Why are we here?';
- to plan the use of meeting time.

To answer 'Why are we here?' the agenda needs to:

- name the topics to be discussed;
- describe them in sufficient detail for each member to understand what precisely is to be discussed;
- refer to or attach back-up papers;
- state the objective behind each agenda item;
- use a clear layout which looks interesting;
- be on one page of A4 paper.

To plan the use of time in the meeting the agenda needs to:

- state the starting and finishing times of the meeting;
- indicate the amount of time to be spent dealing with each agenda item;
- place the items requiring most time at the head of the agenda and those requiring least time at the end;
- be sent out at least three days before the meeting, so that the members can read it and think about what they intend to say;
- contain all the items to be discussed.

*Pitfalls*
- If the agenda is sent out too far ahead, some members will lose it.
- If too many background papers are circulated, the object of

time planning is defeated by the inertia that mountainous reading produces in the participants.

- Remember, if the papers have been circulated, the chairman must have read them!
- 'Any other business' is always an invitation to waste time.

### Agenda layout

**Social Club Committee Meeting**

24 March 1989 10.00 am (finish 11.30 am)

Agenda

| *Item* | *Details* | *Responsible* | *Time allowed* |
| --- | --- | --- | --- |
| 1. | Annual cricket match 20 June 1989<br>To allocate responsibilites<br>To plan timetable of events<br>To plan guestlist | J Allan | 20 minutes |
| 2. | Hall maintenance<br>To decide what to do about: electric hand driers, decorations | R Colbourne | 10 minutes |
| 3. | Skittles meeting 1 March to hear a report on the evening | L Lock | 5 minutes |

## Taking control

### The chairman

A meeting that is out of control is a meeting that can achieve nothing. The meeting will get out of control faster than anything given the following types of chairman:

- *The dictator:* The opportunity of chairmanship is to impose this chairman's will on a group. Chairmanship is to him a licence to dominate. Such chairmanship is a harangue interspersed with demands for group agreement.

- *The scoutmaster:* Collective activity of the group is enough, it does not have to achieve anything. Lots of discussion, lots of positive strokes, very little meeting satisfaction and no achievement.
- *The abdicator:* Either insecure or lazy, this chairman looks to the meeting for support and reassurance, so that the responsibility for indecisiveness can be spread among the group. Every expression of disagreement is seized upon as a way to justify no decision being taken.
- *The persuader:* Talks so much during the meeting that he loses control.
- *The collector:* Listens to ideas, runs the meeting effectively, but collects all the good ideas to himself and promotes them at a later date.
- *The destroyer:* Did not want to take the chair, had the job thrust upon him and now begrudges every moment spent in the meeting. This chairman has an attitude of 'they expect us to do . . . therefore we'll do . . .'.

Compare these chairmen with the effective chairman:

- His source of pleasure in the meeting is the role of achievements from the meeting.
- His role is to assist the group towards the best conclusion or decision in the most efficient manner possible; to interpret and clarify; to move the discussion forward and to bring it to a resolution that everyone understands and accepts as being the will of the meeting, even though individuals do not necessarily agree with it.
- His source of authority with the members is the strength of his perceived commitment to their combined objective, and his skill and efficiency is helping and guiding them to its achievement.
- He uses control and discipline to impose the group's will on any individual who is in danger of diverting or delaying the progress of the discussion away from realisation of the objective.
- He is the impartial servant rather than the committed master of the meeting.

### The advocate

There will be times when the chairman is concerned that a point be strongly presented, times when he does have a commitment to a desired outcome. But the chairman cannot be the one to speak out in this role. He must appoint, as advocate, some member of the group to make the committed speech on his behalf. Often, the role of the advocate goes to the deputy chairman, if such a title exists.

### The recorder

One member of the meeting takes the minutes. The minute taker should not be a visiting outsider, such as the chairman's secretary, but rather a member of the meeting. Such a job requires a reasonable amount of dexterity to ensure that the notetaker gets all the relevant details recorded but does not fail to contribute to the meeting as a result of his recording activities.

The responsibility for the minutes lies with the chairman: he can and must delegate the authority and power to take the minutes, but he remains responsible for their preparation.

## Conducting the meeting

With everyone in position and the agenda lying on the table, the meeting has to commence. The chairman's job is to ensure that the meeting achieves its objectives.

### Structure the discussion

Start by ensuring that every agenda point is discussed efficiently and in such a way as to satisfy all the members. Carry out the five-point plan (see Chapter 7).

- Define the problem/situation complication.
- Quantify the time period. How long has the problem been there?
- Analyse all the information available to get at the facts.
- Establish the options.
- Decide on the action.

*The chairman's tricks*

- Think about each item before the meeting.
- Think out a suggested plan of action.
- If the meeting fails to come up with a five-point plan, suggest your own.

- Allow your own plan to be a devil's advocate, ie let it be altered and adapted as the meeting sees fit.

**Running the meeting**

- Start on time.
- Welcome all the members.
- Introduce any new members.
- Stick firmly to the order of the agenda.
- Obey the timings on the agenda.
- Actively listen to the meeting.
- Deal with the subject.
- Deal with the people.
- Sum up the meeting.
- Conclude the meeting on time.
- Thank members for attendance.

**Dealing with the subject**

- At the start of discussing any item make the objectives clear and indicate where the meeting should get to by the end:
  - — Decision.
  - — Recommendation.
  - — Discussion
  - — Set up further meeting.
  - — Set the scene.
  - — Approve a proposal.
  - — Note the report.
- Ensure that all members understand the issue and why they are discussing it:
  - — Someone may need to make a presentation briefing the meeting.
  - — Explain the story so far.
  - — Discuss what needs to be done next.
  - — Discuss possible lines of enquiry.
  - — List points for and against.
- Clarify complex discussion:
  - — Use a flipchart to illustrate and record points.
  - — Act like a judge and ask for clarification if necessary.
  - — Concentrate fully and be ready to explain.
  - — If you don't understand say so, you will not be alone.
  - — Keep the discussion away from sterile areas.
  - — Ask people for facts and experience to illustrate a point.

  - Make interim summaries.
- Prevent misunderstanding:
  - Watch for the body language that says members do not understand.
  - Ask for explanation yourself.
  - Get translations of jargon used.
  - Make sure all members use the same words to mean the same thing.
- Don't reinvent the camel
  - If the committee has to examine a draft document, take the points for correction and delegate the final corrections to one individual.
- Terminate the discussion in good time
  - As soon as the meeting reaches agreement, confirm that agreement and move on.
- Close discussion before agreement when it becomes clear that:
  - more facts are needed;
  - the views of people not present are needed;
  - more time is needed to think;
  - events are changing and the decision may change;
  - there is not enough time at this meeting to resolve the agenda item properly;
  - it becomes clear that the matter should be dealt with by a working party outside the meeting and merely reported back to the meeting.
- Never terminate the discussion or close the item just because it is a difficult one - the difficulty will not go away.
- Summarise what has been agreed:
  - at the end of each agenda item;
  - as part of the dictation of minutes;
  - to motivate by indicating what has been achieved;
  - to put that achievement on record;
  - to confirm the acceptance of action required by members.

**Dealing with people**

- List all late arrivals in the minutes and don't permit them to interrupt the meeting on arrival.
- Seat people to take advantage of eye-to-eye contact:
  - Sitting face to face over a table enhances conflict.
  - Sitting side by side makes disagreements harder.
  - The seat to the immediate right of the chairman is a 'dead

  - man's corner; the occupant will not be easily seen and involved.
  - The nearer the chairman, the greater the honour.
- Watch the body language to see who is against and who is for the item.
- Control the garrulous, they never notice or mind.
- Draw out the silent:
  - hostility to the chairman;
  - diffidence.
- Protect the weak, they too have good ideas.
- Encourage the clash of ideas: conflict stimulates, but don't let it turn into a fight.
- Watch out for the suggestion squasher: don't squash him but show particular warmth to the suggestion made. Let your disapproval show in your body language.
- Come to the most senior people last. As a rule, the more junior will be less inhibited this way, particularly if the senior person says something that is patently wrong or mistaken.
- Close on a note of achievement; 'thank you' is one of the most useful phrases in the English language.

**Stimulating comment**

Feedback is the only sign you have that the group is still alive out there. The chairman needs feedback to know how the mood of the meeting is developing. If feedback is not forthcoming, and it is important to remember that people can be reluctant to speak out in a group for fear of feeling like idiots, the chairman may need to deliberately stimulate feedback by the use of questions:

- Ask questions that will give you valuable information:
  - 'How are we tackling this problem at the moment?'
  - 'Has anyone had experience of . . .'.
- Ask comparative questions:
  - 'What alternatives are there?'
- Refer to specific individuals:
  - 'I believe, John Brown, you have encountered this problem.'
  - 'I was talking to Margaret Smith earlier and she told me about a problem her department have encountered . . . How, let me see, have I got this right, Margaret?'

Involving the group in this way will:

- keep them awake;
- help their concentration;
- steer the meeting towards a universallly acceptable decision;
- help the chairman relax.

Use questions to provoke the group:

- *To open discussion:* Let them add their facts to those already stated. 'Does anyone have any other experiences?'
- *To develop understanding:* Help them to recall the essential points made so far. 'But, what was the prime drawback ...?'
- *To stimulate thinking:* Arouse the group's curiosity and give them the desire to explore the subject further. 'Suppose . . . , what would we need to do then?
- *To direct thinking:* To bring the meeting back to the point. 'But what about . . . ?'
- *To accumulate information:* Let the group add to the fund of knowledge. 'But, let me ask you, what problems have the various departments found . . . ?'
- *To develop the subject:* A more subtle expansion of the argument. 'Have you considered . . . ?
- *To change the trend of a discussion:* Phrase your question properly and you can draw the group away from areas that will sidetrack them. 'What has been our thinking about . . . ?'
- *To terminate or eliminate discussion:* If one person is dominating the group, cut him off by talking direct to another. 'What have you found to be the root of the problem, Peter?'
- *To arrive at a summary:* A good way of introducing the recommendations. 'Well, where has all that got us to?'
- *To test an argument:* If someone is opposing the chairman or his advocate's suggestions, try to find out the degree of support. 'Let's get things into context, how much importance should we attach to this section, I wonder?'
- *To cut waffle:* Another way of moving on. 'We could go on at length, but what else is there to add that's new on this specific point?'
- *To draw attention to difficulties:* Another way of destroying an alternative argument. 'How much more complex is this problem than we had at first assumed?'

- *To hasten things on:* Suggest that now is the time for action. 'After all, what else can we expect to develop in this area in the next few months?'

To get an answer, make sure that:

- you use a questioning tone;
- you use body language to emphasise the question;
- you pause to wait for a reply (keep your nerve);
- you use what?, why?, where?, when?, who?, how?, so that a straight yes or no is impossible.

## Defusing arguments

It may be necessary to defuse strong argument in the group in the following way:

- 'Of course, we can see that a Rolls-Royce is more difficult to park, nevertheless . . . '
- 'Naturally, the alternative course of action has points to recommend it too.'
- 'Don't let's criticise the alternatives, we merely need to emphasise the ideal solution as we see it . . . '

By pointing out these facts, you give credibility to argument. But always make sure that the limitations of the idea you wish to support are in the first half of the sentence, only to be countered by reaffirmation of the persuasive points in the second half.

## Dealing with questions from the group

Rule number one is:

- If at any time you *don't know* the answer to a question, *say so.*

Offer to come back later with an answer or to find someone who can answer, but *never never* bluff your way out.

Two types of question may come your way:

- *Bombshell question:* 'What relevance can this have to our problems?' This is a difficult, general question, directed not just at the chairman, but generally at the whole group. Use it to start discussion and gradually lead the discussion back to the meeting plan.
- *Rifle-ball question:* 'How will this affect us?' This is a direct question seeking a direct answer. It is often used to check the chairman's knowledge. Answer it and move on. If you don't know the answer, say so, and offer to come back later.

Two techniques will help you out of tricky situations:

- *Backfire the question:* A technique for dealing with the rifle-ball question fired from the group. Bounce it back. 'Well, you tell me how you think it will affect us.'
- *Ricochet the question:* Bounce the question off several people in the group. Let them all try out their views, while you take time to think of the right answer.

## What to do in tricky situations

*Personality clashes*

- Emphasise points of agreement and minimise points of disagreement.
- Draw the group's attention to the purpose of the meeting.
- Bring in someone else.
- Ask the opponents outright to put their differences aside for a moment.

*Side conversation*

- Ask one of the individuals a question.
- Restate the last remark and ask one of the talkers his opinion.
- Carry on and force the meeting to ignore them if possible.
- Try not to embarrass them; let the group tell them to shut up.

Finally, there are eight sure-fire ways to stop achievement in a meeting: don't let them do it.

- *Playing the individual and not the ball*
  - Trying to use discussion to score over an individual.
  - Trying to use emotive pressures such as money or status to persuade.
  - Appealing to envy or prejudice.
  - An argument directed at ignorance from superior knowledge.
- *Argument by analogy*
  - The value of analogy is in inventing more options.
  - The danger of analogy is in extending false analogies and assuming that the decision is made because the solution applies in the analogy.
- *Rationalising*
  - Rationalisation is the asking for reasons where reasons should not apply.

  - The risk of using rationalisation to justify negative attitudes is high.
  - Rationalising can also be a form of buck passing, the invention of scapegoats of one type or another.
- *Drawing irrelevant conclusions*
  - The *non sequitur* of one line of reasoning to another.
  - Red herrings and diversions come in all shapes and sizes, often when the argument is at its weakest.
- *Reduction to absurdity*
  - A good way to destroy a thesis is to reduce it to the absurd.
  - Since the absurd rarely occurs, the argument is self-destructive.
- *No decision/no action*
  - A tempting solution often ushered in with the words 'Leave it till we're not so busy' or 'Let's set up a working party to decide this one.'
  - Making no decision is indeed a clear and valid option, but it may not be the right option.
  - Where it's a case of solution *A* as opposed to solution *B* or no action, and both *A* and *B* bring fewer problems than no action, a decision has to be made.
- *All and some*
  - The abstraction of the infrequent or frequent occurrence to be accepted as the norm.
  - Statistics often lead to all and some errors.
- *Middle of the road*
  - The assumption that truth never lies in extremes is false.
  - Just as is the assumption that there is a link between opposites.

## Taking notes

Meetings should not be held simply for their own sake: they are action gatherings. Consequently their minutes need to reflect the actions taken and those to be taken.

Minutes need to record:

- the time and date of the meeting;
- where it was held;
- who chaired the meeting;
- the names of all present, together with apologies for absence;
- lateness list;

- all agenda items discussed and the decision reached;
- the name of the person responsible for the action;
- any significant points raised in discussion;
- the time at which the meeting ended;
- the date, time and place of the next meeting.

Meetings do *not* need to record:

- every word that was spoken;
- everyone who spoke;
- all the alternative solutions that were not chosen;
- verbatim comments from those in attendance.

Minutes are 'documents of action', *not* a trip down memory lane.

**Action minutes**
For the majority of meetings, the best minutes are action minutes. They have the following additional rules:

- minutes to appear on one page only;
- no waffle;
- full use of headings;
- indication of who is responsible for further action;
- short sentences, simple words.

## Getting the best out of people

To hold a successful meeting, you need to get participation from all those summoned to take part. Some people will be easy to involve, others will be less so, as shown by the following:

*Over-talkative*

| | |
|---|---|
| Why? | May be an eager beaver, a show off, exceptionally well informed or just naturally wordy. |
| What to do | Ricochet questions back. Interrupt with 'What do the rest of the group think?' Let the group keep him under control. |

*Highly argumentative*

| | |
|---|---|
| Why? | May be aggressive personality, professional heckler or someone who is normally good natured and suffering from stress. |
| What to do | Keep your temper. Try to find merit in one of his points. Let the group deal with any obvious misstatements. Try to win his cooperation in any recess. |

*Helpful*

Why? Really tries to help, but often ends up being difficult, as he keeps others out of the discussion.

What to do Cut across him tactfully, by inviting the opinions of others. Thank him and say 'Now let's hear from anyone else with a query.' Let him summarise on your behalf.

*Rambler*

Why? Insecure and unsure of the point he wants to make; he will wander around the topic. He may also like the sound of his own voice.

What to do Wait till he stops for breath and bring in someone else. Smile, agree that his point is interesting but make it clear it is off the subject. Let the group deal with him.

*Obstinate*

Why? A prejudiced individual with an axe to grind. Perhaps he has been thwarted by the organisation and is frustrated and demotivated as a result.

What to do Open his point to the group, let them deal with him. Tell him time is short and you'll be pleased to talk again on the subject on a one-to-one basis later.

*Wrong subject talker*

Why? He may have entirely missed the point. Perhaps less intelligent than the rest, or a sign that you have used too much jargon.

What to do 'I'm sorry, I seem to have misled you; what we need to consider is . . .'

*Complainer*

Why? Perhaps he has a legitimate complaint. A sign that he has been frustrated in achieving his own objectives. Or a professional moaner.

What to do Let someone else in the group take up his point. Point out that you understand his point of view but are powerless to deal with it in a meeting. Turn it to your advantage to illustrate why the proposed idea will be better.

*Inarticulate*

Why? Nervous, less well educated than the rest. Perhaps a junior member of the group.

What to do Never say 'What you mean is . . . '. Say instead, 'Let me put that another way . . . ' Try to twist his ideas as little as possible, but turn them into sense.

*Definitely wrong*

| | |
|---|---|
| Why? | Has not been listening, perhaps prejudiced or ill informed. |
| What to do | 'Well, that is one way of looking at it . . . I see your point, but how can we reconcile it to . . . '. Don't squash him or let the rest of the audience do so. |

*Opinion seeker*

| | |
|---|---|
| Why? | Could be looking for advice or trying to catch you out. Either insecure, a genuine seeker of knowledge or a know-all. |
| What to do | Try never to take sides or the responsibility for someone else's problems. Restate the group's view and emphasise that it is just that. Use him to introduce your summary. |

*Silent minority*

| | |
|---|---|
| Why? | Bored, shy, insecure, indifferent, feels too superior, all are possible. |
| What to do | Try to arouse his interest. Draw out others in the group near him. Ask him a provocative question. Ignore him, you don't need to court problems unless he is someone very important to the meeting. |

## Meetings in a nutshell

To run a successful meeting you need to:

- unite the members at the group in one common purpose;
- focus the attention of the group on the agenda item being dealt with;
- mobilise them into action.

**Unite the group**

The group will not automatically hold a group opinion, or even similar opinions. The problems lie where opposing opinions are strongly held, resulting in aggression and anger among the meeting's members.

Dealing with such agression and anger means that you have to help the group to let off steam while staying neutral as chairman. The trick is to bring in others at the meeting to calm down and defuse the warring sides while ensuring that all stick to the facts.

Opinions only prolong the agony and stir up further dispute. Don't offer your own and don't invite others to do so.

Once the matter has been fully discussed, it's the chairman's job to ensure that the chosen outcome is the right one for the group and that all believe in it and will support it: *United we stand: Divided we fall.*

**Focus the attention of the group**

If members of the group are allowed to stray from the point, the meeting will lose purpose and impetus. It will even cause some members to lose all interest in membership of the group. Don't allow speakers to stray from the point.

The chairman must stay alert: be awake and concentrate throughout the meeting. No one can be allowed to usurp the chairman's role. Never assume everyone has understood, or even been listening. Always check with questions and summaries.

**Mobilise them into action**

The joke that a committee of one is the best committee ignores the fact that more than one opinion is needed to arrive at the best decision or solution. You chose all those members to get the benefit of their contributions; make sure you do get the contributions. Make sure no one gets squashed.

Keep the level of involvement in the group high and the enthusiasm aroused by regular checking around the group for feedback. Maintain eye contact with all your committee - that way they'll feel involved.

One of the most valuable pieces of equipment in a meeting is the flip chart or whiteboard, on to which all ideas can be written and built up into solutions. Use this equipment to get agreed action from the group.

# *Chapter 10*
# Assertiveness

## Types of assertive behaviour

Assertiveness is not about turning the natural mouse into an out of character and unhappy lion; it is about having the confidence to make the right contribution in the right context. It is teaching the mouse to roar when he needs to, but letting him remain in character at all times.

Assertive behaviour is not aggressive behaviour. On the contrary, aggressive behaviour often comes from the same pattern of feelings as non-assertion, as follows:

- Low self-esteem can make you feel vulnerable.
- Feeling vulnerable makes you feel threatened.
- Feeling threatened, you have a choice of behaviour:
  - — attack or aggression
  - — cowering or non-assertive behaviour

both of which lead to stress, something that in its turn leads to less effective management.

People often confuse assertive behaviour with aggressive behaviour, because they think of only one type of assertive behaviour. There are, in fact, several types:

- basic;
- empathetic;
- discrepancy;
- negative feelings;
- consequence;
- responsive.

### Basic

Basic assertive behaviour amounts to a straightforward statement that stands up for your rights by making clear your needs, wants or beliefs. Perhaps you are attending a meeting and the date of the next session is being arranged. You want to attend, but the date everyone else is suggesting would make attendance impossible. Simply say: 'That date means I cannot attend. I should like to do so. The dates I am free on are . . . '

**Empathetic**

Empathetic assertive behaviour contains an element of empathy with the other party in the basic statement of needs or wants. For example, working in a hectic office you need someone's attention even though he is busy, so you say: ' I know you are busy at the moment, David, but I need a quick word with you if I am to get this finished today.'

**Discrepancy**

Discrepancy assertiveness is a statement that points out the differences between what has been previously planned and what has actually occurred. An example may be when someone has failed to complete a task to schedule: 'Mary, when we agreed to tackle this task together, you agreed to give it top priority and to get it done by this afternoon. Now you tell me that you have not got very far and it cannot be completed until next week. I should like to clarify our list of priorities.'

**Negative feelings**

When you feel very upset by what is happening, you may be tempted to become aggressive. Instead, you should use negative feelings assertiveness: a statement that draws the attention of another person to the undesirable effect his behaviour is having on you. The phrases you used are likely to be: When . . . , The effects are . . . , I feel . . . , I'd like . . . . A meeting was due to start at 10.00 am, but two of the key people did not arrive until 10.15 am. You have only just arrived at 10.15 am. The effect of your lateness is to delay the entire meeting and to waste everyone else's time while they wait for you. I'd like an explanation and some kind of guarantee that this will not happen again.'

**Consequence**

Consequence assertiveness is putting the emphasis on the other party. A statement of that nature informs the other party of the consequences to him of not changing behaviour as requested. For example, Fred is habitually late in to work. You decide to deal with the matter: 'Fred, I notice you were late again this morning without any reasonable explanation. This is the third time you have been late this week and the tenth time this month. If this occurs again, I'm left with no alternative but to apply the formal disciplinary procedure. I'd prefer not to. How can I persuade you to change your timekeeping record for the better?'

**Responsive**

Responsive assertiveness will be used when you are trying to negotiate the best action for both parties. It is the way of finding out what the other person wants or needs: his opinions, feelings or stance on the matter. You are planning a change in the office procedures. The change will affect the rate at which work is output and that in turn will affect another department. You say: 'We plan to change our way of doing things to make life in this department more efficient. I realise that our changes may have a knock-on effect on your department. What problems will that create for you?'

## Being more assertive

If you feel you are not as assertive as you should be, you may find the following checklist useful. Copy out the checklist and pin it to the wall above your desk to remind you how to tackle difficult situations when they occur. Here are some general hints on how to be assertive:

- The winner is one who believes he has done well.
- Think positive.
- Rehearse all the good things about life each morning.
- Take a deep breath before taking action.
- Think before communicating.
- Engage brain before thinking.
- Keep looking your best.
- Never say, 'It'll do,' and go out looking a mess.
- Always do your best.
- Never lie to yourself.

The following sections show how to be assertive in certain situations.

## Making requests

- Don't apologise profusely.
- Be direct.
- Keep it short.
- Don't justify yourself.
- Give a reason for your request.
- Don't sell your request.
- Don't play on people's good nature or friendship.
- Don't take a refusal personally.
- Respect the other person's right to say no.

## Refusing requests

- Keep the reply short.
- Tell the truth.
- Don't say, 'I can't'; it sounds like an excuse.
- Acknowledge the requester.
- State limitations or possibilities with total honesty.
- Ask for clarification.
- Ask for time to consider.
- Use body language to emphasise.

## Refusing persistent requests

- Repeat your refusal.
- Don't search for better reasons.
- Don't make excuses.
- State what you want or feel.

## Disagreeing and stating your views

- State disagreement clearly.
- Express doubts in a constructive way.
- Use 'I' to distinguish opinion from fact.
- Change your opinion only in the light of new information.
- Don't be afraid to change your opinion in the light of new information.
- Give reasons for your disagreement.
- State the parts of the whole you disagree with.
- Recognise other people's point of view.

## Giving praise

- Maintain eye contact.
- Keep the praise brief and clear.
- Use 'I' statements.
- Make it specific.

## Receiving praise

- Keep your response short.
- Thank the giver.
- Agree with or accept the praise.
- If you think the praise is wrong, say, 'Thank you,' and then disagree.

## Giving criticism

- Make sure you are not writing a script in your head.
- Make the criticism specific.
- Explain why you want to raise a topic.
- Ask for a response to your criticism.
- Ask for suggestions to bring about change.
- Summarise the suggestions given and endorse them.

## Receiving criticism

- Ask for clarification if you do not understand.
- Do not take criticism as a personal attack.
- If a personal attack is made, draw attention to it and ask for a change.
- If you do not agree say so impersonally and politely.
- Make sure you agree suggestions for the future.
- Keep your voice at normal level.
- Maintain eye contact.
- Don't attack the critic personally.

*Chapter 11*

# Time Management

## Introduction

Time management sounds good, effective and useful, but what does it mean? It is about using time effectively to achieve tasks. Thus, time management is about:

- Prioritising tasks - making lists, evaluating, sorting tasks into categories, judgement.
- Organising yourself - diaries, action lists, booking time for reactive tasks, thinking, planning.

## Time audit

The first step in managing time is to establish just where it has gone. Unless you know what is going awry at the moment, you cannot take the necessary steps to save time. The way to find out is to conduct a personal time audit. This will take time - to save time.

**Find out what you do with your time**

1. Take one typical day and analyse it in detail, describing in a time diary what you do at quarter hourly intervals. (Form 1)
2. About a week to ten days later, take one week and analyse each day in more general terms, detailing what you are doing, once again in quarter hourly intervals. (Form 2)
3. About three days after the initial time audit, group and categorise the tasks listed. (Form 3)
4. From Form 3, decide on answers to the rationale of what you do. (Form 4)
5. Make a checklist of the problem areas, ready to plan and improve them. (Form 5)

## Form 1: Detailed time analysis - one representative day

| *Time* | *Activity* |
| --- | --- |
| 7.00 | |
| 7.15 | |
| 7.30 | |
| 7.45 | |
| 8.00 | |
| 8.15 | |
| 8.30 | |
| 8.45 | |
| 9.00 | |
| 9.15 | |
| 9.30 | |
| 9.45 | |
| 10.00 | |
| 10.15 | |
| 10.30 | |
| 10.45 | |
| 11.00 | |
| 11.15 | |
| 11.30 | |
| 11.45 | |

| *Time* | *Activity* |
| --- | --- |
| 12.00 | |
| 12.15 | |
| 12.30 | |
| 12.45 | |
| 13.00 | |
| 13.15 | |
| 13.30 | |
| 13.45 | |
| 14.00 | |
| 14.15 | |
| 14.30 | |
| 14.45 | |
| 15.00 | |
| 15.15 | |
| 15.30 | |
| 15.45 | |
| 16.00 | |
| 16.15 | |
| 16.30 | |
| 16.45 | |
| 17.00 | |

| *Time* | *Activity* |
| --- | --- |
| 17.15 | |
| 17.30 | |
| 17.45 | |
| 18.00 | |
| 18.15 | |
| 18.30 | |
| 18.45 | |
| 19.00 | |
| 19.15 | |
| 19.30 | |
| 19.45 | |
| 20.00 | |
| 20.15 | |
| 20.30 | |
| 20.45 | |
| 21.00 | |
| 21.15 | |
| 21.30 | |
| 21.45 | |
| 22.00 | |

## Form 2: Detailed time analysis - general terms

| *Time* | *Activity* |
| --- | --- |
| 7.00 | ______ |
| 7.15 | ______ |
| 7.30 | ______ |
| 7.45 | ______ |
| 8.00 | ______ |
| 8.15 | ______ |
| 8.30 | ______ |
| 8.45 | ______ |
| 9.00 | ______ |
| 9.15 | ______ |
| 9.30 | ______ |
| 9.45 | ______ |
| 10.00 | ______ |
| 10.15 | ______ |
| 10.30 | ______ |
| 10.45 | ______ |
| 11.00 | ______ |
| 11.15 | ______ |
| 11.30 | ______ |
| 11.45 | ______ |

| *Time* | *Activity* |
|---|---|
| 12.00 | |
| 12.15 | |
| 12.30 | |
| 12.45 | |
| 13.00 | |
| 13.15 | |
| 13.30 | |
| 13.45 | |
| 14.00 | |
| 14.15 | |
| 14.30 | |
| 14.45 | |
| 15.00 | |
| 15.15 | |
| 15.30 | |
| 15.45 | |
| 16.00 | |
| 16.15 | |
| 16.30 | |
| 16.45 | |
| 17.00 | |

| *Time* | *Activity* |
|---|---|
| 17.15 | |
| 17.30 | |
| 17.45 | |
| 18.00 | |
| 18.15 | |
| 18.30 | |
| 18.45 | |
| 19.00 | |
| 19.15 | |
| 19.30 | |
| 19.45 | |
| 20.00 | |
| 20.15 | |
| 20.30 | |
| 20.45 | |
| 21.00 | |
| 21.15 | |
| 21.30 | |
| 21.45 | |
| 22.00 | |

## Form 3: General terms analysis

Eight activities consume time:

1. *Sleep:* including Sunday post-lunch naps.
2. *Personal:* including washing, dressing, meal times (other than working ones or social ones).
3. *Work travel:* including travel to and from your job as well as travel as part of the job.
4. *Leisure travel:* journeys you make for domestic and leisure reasons.
5. *Domestic responsibilities:* gardening, shopping, housework, etc.
6. *Work* which subdivides into two categories:
   - *Positive active tasks* - planned and organised
   - *Reactive tasks* - reaction to situations.
7. *Self-development:* reading, keeping up knowledge, keep fit etc.
8. *Leisure:* watching TV, playing golf, going out, socialising, etc.

Using the forms, analyse at the end of the day how much time you spent in each category of activities. Next, work out the percentage of the day in each category of activity, as follows:

| *Day* | *Activity code number* | *Percentage* |
|---|---|---|
| 1 | 1 | _____ |
| | 2 | _____ |
| | 3 | _____ |
| | 4 | _____ |
| | 5 | _____ |
| | 6 | _____ |
| | 7 | _____ |
| | 8 | _____ |
| 2 | 1 | _____ |
| | 2 | _____ |

**Form 4: Rationale**

Commonsense tips are the best ways of saving time. But in order to give them, you need to be able to spot the wood from the trees. Read through your time audit sheets to date and answer the following eight questions.

1. What do you do that is unnecessary?

______________________________________________
______________________________________________
______________________________________________
______________________________________________
______________________________________________
______________________________________________

2. What do you do that others could do better (more economically/more effectively)?

______________________________________________
______________________________________________
______________________________________________
______________________________________________
______________________________________________
______________________________________________

3. On which things do you spend too much time?

______________________________________________
______________________________________________
______________________________________________
______________________________________________
______________________________________________
______________________________________________

4. How can you avoid taking too much of other people's time?

______________________________________________
______________________________________________
______________________________________________
______________________________________________
______________________________________________
______________________________________________

5. Where can you make your most important savings?

______________________________________________
______________________________________________
______________________________________________
______________________________________________
______________________________________________
______________________________________________

6. On what do you spend too little time?

______________________________________________
______________________________________________
______________________________________________
______________________________________________
______________________________________________
______________________________________________

7. What are the causes of your time problems?

______________________________________________
______________________________________________
______________________________________________
______________________________________________
______________________________________________
______________________________________________

8. How can you organise more effectively?

______________________________________________
______________________________________________
______________________________________________
______________________________________________
______________________________________________
______________________________________________

**Form 5: Checklist for time improvement**
Fill in below the checklist of problems as shown up by the audit.

*Activity* *Problem/need to change*

______________________________________________________
______________________________________________________
______________________________________________________
______________________________________________________
______________________________________________________
______________________________________________________
______________________________________________________
______________________________________________________
______________________________________________________
______________________________________________________

## How do you waste your time?

To determine how you waste your time, answer the following 20 questions, yes or no:

☐ 1. I delay taking action.
☐ 2. I tend to do things myself instead of delegating.
☐ 3. I don't spend enough time on planning.
☐ 4. I get too involved in details.
☐ 5. I have too few clear cut objectives and goals.
☐ 6. I do not prioritise.
☐ 7. I take too many telephone interruptions.
☐ 8. I waste a lot of time in meetings.
☐ 9. Too many visitors stay too long or are unexpected.
☐ 10. My subordinates are not trained enough.
☐ 11. I don't say 'No' often enough.
☐ 12. I don't have enough time for thinking.
☐ 13. I spend too much time fire-fighting instead of preventing trouble.
☐ 14. Paperwork takes up too much of my time.
☐ 15. Breakdowns in communication take up a lot of time.
☐ 16. I do too much overtime and work too many hours.
☐ 17. I fall behind on deadlines too often.
☐ 18. I don't have enough time to spend with people at work.
☐ 19. I spend too much time moving from place to place.
☐ 20. I have too many things to do.

## Saving time

To save time, you need to think positively. Consider the win/lose syndrome - think to win and you will:

| *A winner says:* | *A loser says:* |
|---|---|
| Let us look into that. | No one knows anything about it. |
| I was wrong. | It was his fault. |
| I was lucky. | I was unlucky. |
| Yes, I will. | Yes, . . . well maybe . . . but . . . |
| I'll make time to do it. | I'm too busy. |
| I'm not afraid of losing. | I'm afraid of winning. |
| Let's get to the point. | Well, it's hard to say exactly. |
| I'll take responsibility for it. | I promise to help. |
| I must have explained it wrongly. | You misunderstood me. |
| I'm sorry, I made a mistake, I'll correct it. | I'm sorry. |
| This isn't worth fighting over. | I won't back down. |
| I'm smart, but could be smarter. | I'm not as stupid as a lot of others. |
| Tell me . . . | As I was saying . . . |
| Let's be friends. | Let me control you. |
| Now he is a man I could learn something from. | He thinks he knows everything. |
| Let me explain. | Let me give you my excuse. |
| What happens over there is my responsibility too. | I only work in this section, not over there. |
| There must be a better way. | This is the way we've always done it. |
| I'd rather be admired than liked. | I'd rather be liked than admired. |

## Time wasters

Time wasters steal time: spot them and stop them. Here are some solutions for common time wasters:

*Poor meetings*

| | |
|---|---|
| Purpose not stated clearly | Draw up an agenda |
| Wrong participants | Only invite those who are needed |
| Too many meetings | Review the results in relation to time spent. Is the meeting really necessary? Use the phone |

| | |
|---|---|
| Poor or no minutes | Write action lists |
| Irrelevant talk | Effective chairmanship |
| No conclusions | Agenda must state decisions to be taken |
| No follow-up | Action lists |
| Indecision | Authority at the meeting |
| Poor chairmanship | Train |
| Not starting on time | Take out a social contract; commit yourself to using the time of others wisely |
| Too many interruptions | Ban them (except for fire or riots) |
| Not sticking to the agenda | Write an action agenda |
| Goes on too long | Take out a social contract |
| *Telephone interruptions* | |
| Conversations too long | Separate chat from information |
| Desire to be available | Train secretary/operator to be selective |
| No plans for unavailability | Schedule a quiet hour |
| Rambling conversation | Plan and list topics to be discussed |
| Need to be involved | Divorce from detail |
| Never ends | Set a social contract at the start |
| Unrealistic time estimates | Use egg timer - when the sand runs out you stop talking |
| Ineffective screening | Train secretary/operator |
| No secretary | Take it in turns to cover for a colleague |
| *Confused responsibility* | |
| Inadequate job description | Make organisation plan with relevant key areas |
| Responsibility without authority | Get necessary authority |
| Inconsistent superior | Politely point out problem |
| Power struggles in organisation | Clarify key areas and co-ordinate |
| Job description overlaps others | Identify and eliminate |
| Usurping of authority by others | If authority is in doubt limit responsibility |
| Ambiguous instruction | Ask for repeat or in writing |

| | |
|---|---|
| *Lack of priorities* | |
| Don't know how | Use the system |
| Lack time to plan | Plan time to have time |
| Lack self-discipline | Establish key areas and tasks, schedule activities for one month, monitor progress |
| Rather move than think | Think before you move |
| No job description | Define key areas |
| *Poor communication* | |
| Don't know they need to know | Determine real needs |
| Language difficulties | Don't use jargon |
| Ignored | Use the right media |
| Unread | Get timing right |
| Long memos and speeches | Cut waste, do not repeat |
| Lack of receptiveness | Active listening |
| Indecision/delay in replies | Send an unless-I-hear memo |
| *Indecision and procrastination* | |
| Lack of faith in decision-making process | Systemise data collection and evaluation for accuracy and reliability |
| Addicted to facts | Use 80/20 rule (see page 92) |
| Lack techniques to improve | Set deadline objectives/ priorities |
| Fear of mistakes | Avoid blame; be constructive |
| Unrealistic time plan | Everything takes longer than you think; allow 20 per cent free time |
| Postponing the unpleasant | Do it first, the rest of the day can't be worse! |
| *Crisis management* | |
| Lack of priorities | Rules to define what is really urgent |
| Doing too much | Say no |
| Lack of foresight | Contingency plans |
| Failure to anticipate | Expect the unexpected (think) |
| Overplanning | Leave 20 per cent of the day free |
| Overreacting | Ignore or delegate or deal |
| Overlooking possible negative consequences of a decision | Anything can go wrong; set up a contingency plan |

| | |
|---|---|
| *Inability to say no* | |
| Desire to help others | You'll be taken for granted |
| Desire to win approval | You may lose respect |
| Fear of offending | Say no nicely |
| Not knowing how | Practise |
| Lack excuse | No excuse is better than a lie |
| Fear that excuse may not justify saying no | Don't always need to be justified |
| Lack of objectives/priorities | Establish key areas and tasks |
| Desire to be productive | Do less and do it well |
| Others assume you will say yes | Start to say no now |
| *Involved in too many things* | |
| Unclear priorities | Specify goals and tasks |
| Overambitious | Display results in important areas |
| Unrealistic time estimates | Everthing takes longer; allow time |
| Action orientated | Don't confuse motion with progress; work effectively, not harder |
| Understaffed | Is that really so? Reallocate tasks |
| Overdemanding job or boss | Make constructive suggestions |
| *Not finishing assignments* | |
| Lack of time limits | Set deadlines |
| Allowing too many interruptions | Set quiet hour |
| No overall perspective | Think about yourself and your job |
| Failure to reward yourself | Defer diversions until task done |
| Too much to do | Drop old responsibilities before taking on new |
| Laziness | Impose a deadline and tell others |
| *Lack of self discipline* | |
| Lack of performance | Impose demands on yourself |
| Postponing the unpleasant | Do it first |
| Lack of direction | Say no to the unimportant |
| Reactive response | Ignore problems that will go away by themselves; delegate others |
| Not follow up | People do what you inspect |

| | |
|---|---|
| Not utilising available tools and techniques | Think before you act |
| Unrealistic time estimates | Allow for your misjudgements |
| Inability to say no | Say no |
| Carelessness | Do it right first time - do it once |
| Tired, out of condition | Keep fit, exercise |
| *Too much reading* | |
| Unclear and poorly edited material | Improve organisation systems |
| Poor reading skill | Recognise and take a course |
| No priorities | List what must be read, assign time |
| *Drop-in visitors* | |
| How to handle? | Develop screening plan |
| Always visible | Find a hideaway; set quiet hour |
| Making decisions below your level | Delegate |
| Expecting subordinates to check with you excessively | Manage by exception |
| Inability to terminate visits | Go to their office and remain standing |
| *Too much routine work* | |
| Lack of priorities | Establish and stick with them |
| Fear of subordinates' mistakes | Train and monitor |
| Fear of losing influence | Re-examine your values |
| I do this job better | Train others |
| *Too much paperwork* | |
| Poor communicating | Use right media |
| Poor administrative rules | Loosen control, make it informal |
| Poor organisation | Standardise/systemise |
| *Personal disorganisation* | |
| Lack of system | Organise yourself |
| Ego (I'm a vital link) | Don't fool yourself, you're not fooling others |
| Fear of forgetting | Write notes |
| Failure to delegate | Learn |
| Procrastination/indecision | 80 per cent of the tasks on your desk can be handled at once, do so |
| Paper blockade, memo-itis | Emphasise brevity |

## Prioritising tasks

The art of prioritising is to select the most important tasks from those waiting in your in-tray. The trick is to know which are important and which merely seem to be important. There is only one way the tasks can be effectively judged: do they go towards achieving the objectives of the organisation as a whole? Such tasks are nearly always important

This, of course, begs the question, What are the objectives of your organisation? Every organisation is set up with a purpose: for the majority it is to make a profit by selling goods or services to clients or customers. For the non-profit making organisation, the objective is usually to collect funds to give to the desired cause or to break even while achieving a cause. Whatever the organisation, it must have an aim and that aim must be made clear to all.

### Active positive tasks

These are tasks that you must do to achieve the objectives of your job. They are the long-term thinking-based tasks. To identify an active positive task look for something that:

- is productive;
- is creative;
- gets results;
- sets the pattern for the future;
- earns you praise and reward.

### Reactive tasks

These tasks are the problems etc that land on your desk every day and have to be dealt with to keep things running. Although reactive tasks are often seen to be urgent, they rarely solve anything. Nor are they creative; but they will expand to fill all your time unless you control them.

### Urgent tasks

Either active positive tasks or reactive tasks can be urgent. The degree of urgency needs to be established in comparison with:

- a scale suitable for you;
- other tasks in the queue.

### Important tasks

These tasks are most likely to be the active positive tasks although some reactive tasks can be important. Don't be misled by the degree of urgency attached to a reactive task; it may be urgent but not important.

Important tasks deserve a lot of time and should not suffer at the hands of urgent ones. The only way to ensure the right balance of time between the two types of task is to categorise and prioritise them. Having done that, you can turn to your diary and book out time for the active positive tasks while leaving space for the reactive ones that you know will inevitably crop up each day.

### Task categorisation

List all the uncompleted tasks in your in-tray, including those that are merely objectives in your overall plan. Now allocate R for reactive, A for active positive, U for urgent and I for important.

| *Task* | *Category* |
| --- | --- |
| | |
| | |
| | |
| | |
| | |
| | |
| | |
| | |
| | |
| | |

## Organising yourself

Organising yourself means keeping in control of diaries, action lists, your desk and the key areas of your life. It means thinking and planning, even booking time to spend time with yourself.

### Key tasks

Knowing the key areas of your job will follow naturally from your time audit and the examination of the reactive and active positive tasks. The key areas should fall easily into place. If you are not sure, consider the following responsibilties:

- responsibility for people;
- responsibility for budgets or finance;
- responsibility for organisational development;
- responsibility for administration;
- responsibility for external communication;
- responsibility for long-term planning.

*People*

Who are you responsible for?

- yourself
- your family
- your subordinates
- your department.

*Finance*

What money are you responsible for?

- your own
- the department
- budgeting
- authorisation of cheques
- authorisation of bought invoices.

*Development*

Whose development is your responsibility?

- the organisation
- the department
- your own
- your family
- creative new ideas.

*Adminstration*

What administration is under your control?

- your office
- your secretary's office
- your department
- your family
- other people's departments
- customers' businesses.

*Communication*
What communication is under your control?

- customer liaison
- selling
- ordering
- internal
- face to face
- instruction
- advice
- family.

*Long-term planning*
Do you have any responsibilities for the future?

- the organisation
- the department
- your life
- your career
- your family.

You will probably find that there are up to nine key areas in your life. Don't forget any of the aspects of them that belong in your leisure and private life. It is not a sign of good time management to be totally work orientated.

Now group the key tasks within the key areas into the categories of reactive and active positive tasks. This is your outline for the planning of your days and your diary.

**Key areas list**
For each of your key areas (up to nine), fill in the following:

| *Objectives* | *Activities* | *Deadlines* | *Responsibility* |
|---|---|---|---|
| | | | |
| | | | |
| | | | |
| | | | |
| | | | |
| | | | |
| | | | |
| | | | |
| | | | |

## Action plan 1: a day

8.00 ______________________
8.30 ______________________
9.00 ______________________
9.30 ______________________
10.00 ______________________
10.30 ______________________
11.00 ______________________
11.30 ______________________
12.00 ______________________
12.30 ______________________
13.00 ______________________
13.30 ______________________
14.00 ______________________
14.30 ______________________
15.00 ______________________
15.30 ______________________
16.00 ______________________
16.30 ______________________
17.00 ______________________
17.30 ______________________
18.00 ______________________
18.30 ______________________
19.00 ______________________
19.30 ______________________
20.00 ______________________
20.30 ______________________
21.00 ______________________
21.30 ______________________
22.00 ______________________

*Tasks*

______________________

*Speak to/write to*

______________________

*Don't forget*

## Action plan 2: plan a week at a time

| *Meetings* | *Must do* | *Thinking* | *Speak/write* |
|---|---|---|---|
| | | | |
| | | | |
| | | | |
| | | | |
| | | | |

## Filling in the action plans

1. Consult your key areas list and for each key area list all the activities necessary to achieve the objectives set.
2. Go through the entire list and set realistic deadlines.
3. Go through the list and decide on your delegation programme for the key areas.
4. Fill in the following on your action day plan:
   - at least half an hour's thinking time a day;
   - one quiet hour per day;
   - spots for the reactive tasks at the optimum time;
   - the key area tasks that you have allotted to yourself, taking heed of your deadlines.
5. Remembering all the time who you are:
   - optimistic or pessimistic;
   - lazy or overactive;
   - thorough or broadbrush approach type;
   - cautious or ambitious;
   - lark or owl.

## Dealing with paper

Paperwork has a tendency to take over in at least three places: the in-tray, the desk and the briefcase.

### *The in-tray*

Take the right attitude to your in-tray from the start:

- If you have a secretary, do not touch your in-tray until she has sorted it.
- If you don't have a secretary or a subordinate capable of dealing with the initial sweep at your in-tray, make the rule to touch each piece of paper once only.

Sort everything into three piles:

- *Action:* may mean a phone call, a visit, a letter, a meeting. As soon as you know it needs action, book it into the action plan.
- *Information:* If it is information for long-term use, file it where you can find it. If it is of passing interest, read it and throw it away. If you want to pass it on, do so now.
- *Dead:* Put all dead material straight into the waste-paper basket.

Don't have a fourth pile, invisibly labelled 'too difficult'. If you need help, ask for it. If it is just difficult, tackle it first; then it will be over.

Remember, you don't want your in-tray filled, so don't fill other people's in-trays unnecessarily.

*Filing*

Filing something where you can find it usually means filing according to ideas and contents, not according to sender. So, many people seem to forget that paper is made from trees and trees are heavy. Why keep a tree when you can keep an idea! If it is the idea you want, transfer it to a small desk top card index and throw the long letter away.

*The desk*

If your desk is clear and welcoming, the new day will feel the same. If your desk is untidy and unwelcoming, you will spend hours looking for a piece of paper.

The following desk rules will help you:

- Set up a system and stick to it.
- File in a filing system.
- Equip your desk with what you need.
- Site your desk in the best place - light and visible to others.
- Make sure your desk and its chair are comfortable.
- Get a desk that is neither too big nor too small.
- Use charts to store information on the wall.
- Keep the telephone in sight and with a notepad.
- Keep regularly consulted documents and book near the desk, not on it.
- Keep the contents of the drawers under control.
- Site the waste-paper basket near the desk so you use it.

A desk management system consisting of six drawers can control all the paper, labelled as follows:

- Do now - papers that you plan to deal with today.
- Do soon - papers that will be worked on within a week.
- File - for your secretary or you when you programmed time.
- Read - don't just let this pile up; if you haven't read it within a week of arrival and it is not programmed into the action plan, pass it on unread to someone who will read it, and ask for feedback.
- Pass on - for things that need to be passed on with a verbal explanation; set up folders for each person and book time in your action plan.
- Awaiting information - don't let it wait for ever; review regularly and send out chase-up notes.

*The briefcase*

Briefcases fill up with rubbish very easily. Every good intent begins with loading the briefcase with work that will be done on the train. Trains are overheated and most business people fall asleep within 10 minutes. Here are some briefcase rules:

- You only need to take papers home if you intend to work on them.
- You only need to take papers to a meeting if you intend to use them.
- You only need to carry magazines with you if you intend to read them.
- You only need a briefcase if you need to carry papers with you.

**How to organise your life better**

1. Go through the list of time wasters and identify those that you think are the most relevant to you - at home and at work.
2. Conduct a time audit regularly to control how you spend time.
3. Compare your updated time audit with your first time wasters' list.
4. Mark the time wasters for killing off one at a time.
5. Manage your desk.
6. Delegate.
7. Communicate effectively.
8. Use the action plan.
9. Keep information in charts.
10. Think and plan ahead.

## Golden rules for good time management

1. Develop a fixed daily routine; do routine things at routine times.
2. Do the important jobs when you are at your best (lark or owl).
3. Set time limits and stick to them.
4. Never put off unpleasant or difficult tasks if they are also important.
5. Put off everything that is not important.
6. Analyse interruptions; take steps to avoid them.
7. Set up a quiet hour and publicise it.
8. Do one thing at a time.
9. Plan phone calls and stick to the plan.
10. Keep a notebook to collect ideas in one place.
11. Wherever possible, finish your task.
12. Arrange breaks at times when you cannot work effectively.
13. Communicate routine matters at routine meetings.
14. Learn to say no.
15. Do similar type jobs at the same time, eg all phone calls one after another.
16. Conduct a time audit about once every four months.
17. Only take work home if you intend to do it.
18. Think, then act.
19. Do things adequately; don't be a perfectionist.
20. Set a task for the year, the month, the week, the day.
21. Make lists and cross off tasks when done; it feels good.

*Chapter 12*

# Making a Presentation

## Planning

A presentation is the communication of ideas by means of words and visual aids. It is more than just talking to a meeting; making a presentation is nearer to a performance designed to make a lasting impression on the audience.

The presentation may be made to a very small group, possibly even to just one person, but the end result will be worth the trouble taken to tailor the information and its delivery to the needs of the listener.

Presentations are likely to be in the following areas:

- persuade
- sell
- convince
- inform
- relieve concern.

The stated purpose may fall into one category and the hidden purpose into another.

All presenters need to provide the answer to five questions before starting to write the presentation:

- Why?
- What?
- Who?
- Where?
- How?

### Why?

Never start preparation for a presentation without first considering all the purposes involved. The hidden purpose may, in fact, be more important than the declared one. Informing, for example, very rarely stands alone; it is usually also required to persuade the audience to accept and use the information given.

- Define clearly and in writing all the objectives of the presentation.
- Try out your stated objectives on anyone else involved to make quite sure they are accurate. Mistakes at this stage will result in presentations that miss the mark.
- Keep the objectives in front of you at all times during the writing of and preparation of the presentation. Write them firmly on the front of your notes to make sure that, in the heat of the moment, you do not deviate from your stated purpose.

## What?

Quite simply, what are you going to say? It is easy to know what you want to say, when the idea first presents itself, but far harder when the time comes to write down the text of a proposed presentation.

- Keep a presentation notebook and jot down all connected ideas as they occur. Don't worry about order, simply get them on to paper so that they are not forgotten.
- Think in visual terms. Make notes or sketches of visual aids that might be used. Consider actual physical items to introduce.
- Keep the notebook open as long as possible. That is, don't write off an idea because it has come too late; be prepared to revise and adjust right up to the last possible moment.

## Who?

If you don't know who you are talking to, you will have no idea of their likes, dislikes, prejudices or background knowledge.

- Never make assumptions about an audience. Base your knowledge on facts.
- For an in-house audience, finding the facts means turning to the personnel files or asking heads of department.
- For an external audience, it may mean asking for names and looking up information, finding out past experiences in your area, establishing what your audience do at present. And that may mean making phone calls to secretaries, reading existing client files, asking them for advance information, talking to your audience in advance.
- Never be afraid to ask for information; it simply shows that you care enough to detail the presentation to the actual audience.

- Wherever possible, arrange to chat to the audience over coffee or tea or drinks just before beginning the presentation, so that you can make accurate references to them throughout the presentation.
- Find a way of remembering names. If you have a bad memory, go on a memory skills course. Remembering names and personal information makes all the difference in any presentation.

**Where?**

Don't start to plan anything until you know where you are going to make your presentation. If it is to be on unfamiliar territory, it may not be possible to find out total detail, but you do need to know certain crucial facts.

- Where is the venue? How do you get there and how long will the journey take? Allow too much time.
- What facilities are available at the venue - overhead projector, flipchart, 35-mm slide projector, video equipment, lectern?
- What type of lighting is possible?
- What is the seating like?
- Where will you stand?
- What is the noise level likely to be?
- Find out where all the facilities are.
- Find out where the offices of people you may need are.
- If you cannot visit the venue, make a phone call or write a letter to get the information you need. Once again, don't be afraid to ask; people prefer to get it right and appreciate your concern.

**How?**

You know what, to whom, why and where but you don't yet know how you are going to put over your message. Much of the 'how' will depend on the answers to the previous four questions. The most wonderful presentation will fail if it misses the level of the audience, or the room is too light to see slides, or you don't have a plan. The answer to how is in foreknowledge of the conditions and having a plan.

- Take all the knowledge and plan the presentation down to the last detail.
- Don't be over-ambitious or impractical. If conditions mean the idea won't work, it won't work. Get a new idea or change the conditions.

- Convince yourself. If you don't sound convinced, you don't stand a chance of convincing others.
- Get ideas into the best order possible and don't deviate.
- Write as fully detailed notes as you need. Not just speaking notes, but general plans for the presentation and how things will run.

## Preparation

Preparation means knowing the facts. The facts as they stand, the facts as you wish to present them, the facts the audience want to know and the facts the audience need to know.

Preparation also means selecting your audience, if that is possible, or at the least knowing your audience.

Preparation also includes rehearsal. No matter how small or simple the presentation it will be better for a rehearsal.

### Facts

Facts fall into several categories. You need to know them all in order to present effectively.

- The real and total facts relating to the situation.
- The facts not precisely relevant but affected by the situation.
- The plus factors, ie the facts in your favour.
- The negative factors, ie the facts against your case.
- The facts the audience want to hear, ie the level of acceptance of the truth.
- The facts the audience know already.
- The facts the audience need to know, as opposed to the ones they think they need to know.

Take all the facts and categorise them according to the above. Knowledge is half the battle. If you know the facts, you can manipulate them and use them to your own ends. If they take you by surprise, even when in your favour, they can work against you.

### Audience

If you have the opportunity to select your audience, use it. That does not mean that you should always aim to preach only to the converted; rather that you should be able to plan the right level of presentation for the audience.

Audience selection criteria are as follows:

- Individuals with the same basic knowledge level. Otherwise everyone will get frustrated for part of the time.
- Individuals with the same user requirement. So you can concentrate your presentation effectively.
- Individuals with a variety of user requirements. So you can demonstrate the versatility of your idea.
- Individuals from mixed disciplines. So you can be sure of varied input.
- Individuals who mix well together. So you do not suffer from inhibited audiences.

If you cannot select your audience, and that is normally the case, make sure you know who they are.

- Take time to find out names and backgrounds, even just at the start of a presentation.
- Make eye contact with them all and keep it.
- Watch for reactions and body language all the time.
- Be flexible in your presentation and try to react to the audience.

Whoever picked your audience, and whomsoever they are, if you make them feel that you care, they will respond to you. Here are some hints:

- smile;
- relax, if possible;
- admit any mistake;
- don't be arrogant or dismissive;
- listen to questions and comment;
- be nice.

**Rehearsal**

The second time you do anything tends to be better than the first. First time around you learn what needs to change, second time you put it right.

Every presenter needs enough adrenalin to make the presentation, but not so much that stress occurs. Rehearsal will take the stress out of a presentation.

- Rehearse the whole presentation, not just bits of it.
- Wherever possible, rehearse *in situ,* or at least in a realistic replica.

- Make sure you know how to work all the equipment.
- Rehearse using the visual aids you have planned.
- Rehearse walking to and from your presentation spot.
- Check on what you intend to wear. This is often a problem for women. Try to wear things that give you confidence without imposing their own problems and constraints.

**Back-up**

What happens if you fall under a bus? Or get flu? Make sure there is someone able to take your place in the presentation. Perhaps they are not well rehearsed, but they should know the material and how it is to be presented. Another reason for the presenter's notebook. Ideas in heads stay there when heads die; ideas in notebooks go on for ever and provide a living memorial!

## Talking

Much of the presentation is about talking to an audience. Talking really amounts to three things:

- the structure of the presentation;
- vocabulary and speaking ideas;
- the act of opening and closing the presentation, ie the memorable bits.

**Structure**

The structure of every good presentation will be the same. That is, six logical steps, one moving to the next:

- *Preface*
  - — The opening courtesies.
  - — Introduction of the presenter.
  - — A statement of the purpose of the presentation.
  - — Details of the duration and shape of the presentation.
  - — The rules of the road.
- *Position*
  - — A brief outline of the present situation.
- *Problem*
  - — A description of the audience need.
  - — A statement of the fact that your proposal can meet that need.

- *Possibilities*
  - — A look at all the alternatives.
  - — Plus factors first.
  - — Then negative factors.
  - — Reiterating the plus factors.
- *Proposal*
  - — A statement of the recommended course of action.
- *Postscript*
  - — A summary of the proposal.
  - — The next step the audience need to take.
  - — Description of any supporting documentation.
  - — Thanks.
  - — Invitation to ask questions.

## Vocabulary

- A presentation need not use such formal language as a report. Nor need it be as carefully worded as a speech.
- Avoid jargon terms unless you are certain that the entire audience understands their meaning.
- Avoid slang, but use colloquial phrases.
- Keep sentences short.
- Head up and good diction are essential.

## Opening and closing a presentation

The most memorable remarks made at any presentation are the opening remarks and the closing ones.

- Keep them short and punchy.
- Make sure they relate to the subject.
- Make sure they put over your chosen argument.
- Lift your voice while making them.
- Smile while making them.
- Use body language to emphasise them.
- Make sure you are confident when you start.
- Close on a high note, don't just fade away.

## Delivery

Most people speak well enough to friends and colleagues; it is only when they know that they are faced with a 'performance' that they go to pieces. Adrenalin is essential when speaking; stress is bad news.

Adrenalin is the hormone which provides the sense of tension caused by reaction to circumstances. Without adrenalin we are not afraid. Without fear we rarely perform well. A good presenter needs enough nervousness to concentrate the mind on the presentation being made. For this reason it is important to have sufficient when speaking. Too much adrenalin, however, can physically lock the muscles. It can cause the mind to go completely blank even when speaking well rehearsed material. For this reason we need to relax sufficiently to withdraw the stress element but keep the tension so that the drive and spirit remains.

Keep the adrenalin and conquer the stress by using breathing and relaxation exercises.

- Start off right; breathing and relaxation exercises.
- Don't mumble; too loud is better than unheard.
- Don't hesitate; 'er' is the most irritating word in the English language.
- Don't gabble; paced speech will be understood.
- Beware of catch phrases; if they become too frequent, they will distract the audience.
- Maintain eye contact at all times; keep looking from one to another, never look at the screen behind you or at the floor.
- Keep mannerisms under control; they can be a distraction.
- Never drop your voice at the end of a sentence; you want to be heard at all times.

## Exercises for voice and speech

*Relaxation*

1. Shake fingers, wrists, and extend to elbows and finally shoulders. Shake right leg, left leg. Feel that you are getting rid of all your tensions.
2. Allow head to fall forwards by relaxing neck muscles. Roll head round several times, bending slightly from the waist so that the weight of the head takes it round. Stop and rotate slowly in the opposite direction several times. Come to rest, chin on chest.
3. Repeat the exercise keeping the shoulders still and rotating head similarly only using the neck muscles to send it round. Do not use more tension than is required for the job.
4. Sag, allowing head to fall forwards, chin on chest, deflate whole chest, relax stomach wall, bend at knees. Now you are in a wrong position. Beginning with the feet, weight forwards on the balls of the feet, straighten the legs, stomach wall

under control, expand the whole chest, first lower chest, then upper chest, shoulders held back, finally bring the head into the horizontal.

Get out of the wrong position in order to be in the right position.

*Breathing and voice*

1. Sigh heavily allowing the chest to collapse. Repeat
2. Inhale by raising the floating ribs and drawing air into the chest. Count. Keep ribs lifted throughout. Should they fall between counts draw breath in by extending floating ribs by muscular action. This is called topping up.

As you breathe count aloud. At the first attempt, you will probably only manage 1 to 5 on breathing in and 6 to 10 on breathing out. With practice, you should be able to build up to 1 to 25 on breathing in and 26 to 50 on breathing out. Count on one note using the middle range of the voice with fully sustained tone and releasing the voice fully and freely.

*Resonance*

| | |
|---|---|
| Hum: | ---mmmmm--- crescendo and diminuendo |
| Sustain: | moo... moh... maw... mah... may...me... |
| Sing: | Mary had a little lamb |
| Say: | I must keep my voice at the front of my mouth |

*Tongue*

Protrude tongue, pointing it, withdraw and repeat to the left, to the front, to the right, to the front, and so on.

*Articulation*

This is a form of gymnastics between the tip of the tongue, the teeth and the lips. Practice: *red leather yellow leather*.

*Improve your vocal range*

| | | |
|---|---|---|
| 1. | It's a wonderful day | high pitch |
| 2. | It's a lovely day | |
| 3. | It's a nice day | middle pitch |
| 4. | It's a miserable day | |
| 5. | It's a horrid day | low pitch |

Speak in order 3, 2, 1, back to 3, then 4, 5.

Here is a poem to practise your vocal range. Begin on a low note and raise the pitch in each succeeding line:

Hark to the trump and the drum
And the mournful sound of the barb'rous horn
And the flap of the banners that flit as they're borne
And the neigh of the steed and the multitude's hum
And the clash and the shout
They come! They come!

**Detail**

How much detail should you go into?

- If the subject is really complicated, it probably needs very detailed back-up notes and therefore you can keep the detail in your presentation to a minimum.
- If the audience knows a great deal about the subject, beware of falling into detailed arguments, so use 'As you will realise, I don't have time to go into great detail, but I think we would all consider a generalisation of 40 per cent to be reasonable . . . .'
- If the audience knows nothing about the subject, detail will only serve to confuse the issue. Once again it is better in a handout.

In other words - in doubt? - leave it out.

**Getting feedback**

Feedback is the only sign you have that the audience is still alive out there. You need feedback to know how the session is progressing. If you really want to convince or persuade, you will need to take questions. If feedback is not forthcoming, and it is important to remember that people can be reluctant to speak out in a group for fear of feeling like idiots, go out and seek it yourself by the use of questions:

- Ask questions that will give you valuable information:
  - 'How are you tackling this problem at the moment?'
  - 'Has anyone had experience of . . . .'
- Ask comparative questions:
  - 'What alternatives have you considered?'
- Refer to specific individuals:
  - 'I believe, John Brown, you have encountered this problem.'

'I was talking to Margaret Smith in the coffee break, and she told me about a problem her company have encountered . . . Now, let me see, have I got this right, Margaret?'

Involving the audience in this way will:

- keep them awake;
- help their concentration;
- help you relax.

Don't forget to be magnanimous about the alternatives to your idea and the shortfalls your idea may have, as in the following.

- 'Of course, I realise that a Rolls-Royce is more difficult to park . . . .'
- 'Naturally, the alternative course of action has points to recommend it too.'
- 'Far be it for me to criticise the alternatives, I merely want to emphasise the ideal solution as I see it . . . .'

By pointing out these facts, you give credibility to your arguments. But always make sure that the limitations of your idea are in the first half of the sentence, only to be countered by reaffirmation of the persuasive points in the second half.

*Using questions*
Use questions to help you deal with the audience:

- *To open discussion:* Let them add their facts to your own. 'Does anyone have any other experiences?'
- *To develop understanding:* Help them to recall the essential points you made. 'But, what was the prime drawback . . . ?'
- *To stimulate thinking:* Arouse the audience's curiosity and give them the desire to explore the subject further. 'Suppose ..., what would we need to do then?'
- *To direct thinking:* To bring the meeting back to the point you want to consider. 'But what about . . . ?'
- *To accumulate information:* Let the audience add to your fund of knowledge. 'But, let me ask you, what problems have you found ... ?'
- *To develop the subject:* A more subtle expansion of the argument. 'Have you considered . . . ?'
- *To change the trend of a discussion:* Phrase your question properly and you can draw the audience away from areas you

do not wish to explore. 'What has been your thinking about . . . ?'
do not wish to explore. 'What has been your thinking about ...?'

- *To terminate or eliminate discussion:* If one person is dominating the question session, cut him off by talking direct to another. 'What have you found to be the root of the problem, Mr Jones?'
- *To arrive at a summary:* A good way of introducing your recommendations. 'Well, where has that got us to?'
- *To test an argument:* If someone is opposing you from the floor, try to find out the degree of support (NB. It might be better to move on, but you would lose some credibility.) 'Let's get things into context, how much importance should we attach to this section, I wonder?'
- *To imply that all there is to be said has been said:* Another way of moving on. 'I could go on at length, but what else is there to say on this specific point?'
- *To draw attention to difficulties:* Another way of destroying an alternative argument. 'How much more complex is this problem than we had at first assumed?'
- *To hasten things on:* Suggest that now is the time for action. 'After all, what else can we expect to develop in this area in the next few months?'

All these questions may be actual questions or rhetorical ones. Either way they will personalise the presentation.

If you want to answer, make sure that:

- you use a questioning tone;
- you use body language to emphasise the question;
- you pause to wait for a reply (keep your nerve);
- you use what?, why?, where?, when?, who?, how?, so that a straight yes or no is impossible.

If you don't want an answer:

- don't pause after the question, keep the structure flowing;
- don't use a questioning tone;
- make it clear from your body language that you are about to answer the self-imposed question;
- use 'but' or 'however' to open the question.

If you want an argument:

- posing the question, 'What do you think?' will stand a good

chance of getting you one;
be careful to keep control when seeking opinions.

*Dealing with questions from the audience*
Rule number one is:

- If at any time you *don't know* the answer to a question, *say so.*

Offer to come back later with an answer or to find someone who can answer, but *never* bluff your way out.
Two types of question may come your way:

- *Bombshell question:* 'What relevance can this have to our problems?' This is a difficult, general question, directed not just at the speaker, but generally at the whole group. Use it to start discussion and gradually lead the discussion back to your planned session.
- *Rifle-ball question:* 'How will this affect us?' This is a direct question seeking a direct answer. It is often used to check the speaker's knowledge. Answer it and move on. If you don't know the answer, say so, and offer to come back later.

Two techniques can be used to deal with audience questions:

- *Backfire the question:* Not so much a question, more a technique for dealing with the rifle-ball question fired from the audience. Bounce it back. 'Well, you tell me how you think it will affect us?' A good way of playing for time or dealing with a 'know-all'.
- *Ricochet the question:* Bounce the question off several people in the audience. Let them all try out their views, while you take time to think of your answer.

## Visual aids

It is possible to ruin a good presentation by failing to illustrate with visual aids. Too many visual aids, on the other hand, particularly if they are of various types, will confuse and distract from the speaker. If you are going to use them, use them well.

**Why should you use visual aids?**
People remember very little of what they hear, only about 20 per cent of information disseminated by spoken methods is retained; add visual input and the retention can be as high as 80 per cent. So,

use visual aids to enhance the things you want the audience to remember, and leave unillustrated the things you want them to forget.

The possible types of visual aid are:

- charts
- graphs
- lists
- pictures
- cartoons
- quotations
- physical objects
- actual dramatised events
- role plays.

Most of these can be presented in the following forms:

- flipcharts
- black or whiteboards
- prepared charts
- overhead projection slides
- 35-mm slides
- films
- videos.

## When to use what

- Allow yourself to be restricted by the surroundings.
- Don't be over-ambitious.
- Stick to no more than one or possibly two types of visual aid in a short presentation.
- Let the material dictate the media.
- Be aware of the audience and their needs.

The easiest and cheapest aid to use is prepared overhead projection slides, which:

- are effective;
- can be used in daylight;
- require easily transportable equipment;
- can reproduce most ideas clearly;
- use colour;
- let the speaker maintain eye contact.

The most effective but more expensive aid is purpose-made 35-mm slides or video presentations, which:

- are effective;
- can reproduce ideas very clearly;
- use colour;
- let the speaker maintain eye contact;
- are exciting.

On the other hand, such presentations:

- are costly to produce;
- require cumbersome equipment;
- need a darkened room for 35 mm slides, as for some videos;
- can seem rather too professional and so appear as a hard sell.

The most effective aids but with drawbacks are videos and films on related subjects, which:

- are effective;
- can reproduce ideas very clearly;
- use colour;
- let the speaker maintain eye contact;
- are exciting and often funny.

On the other hand, these:

- are more a training aid;
- involve hire or purchase costs;
- require cumbersome equipment;
- need a darkened room.

The worst possible choices of aid are flipcharts, blackboards or whiteboards on their own because:

- the speaker loses eye contact;
- flipcharts are noisy to turn over;
- boards are messy to use;
- the number of prepared messages is restricted.

**Using the visual aids**

- Check them through to make sure they are all there, in the right order and usable.
- Check the equipment.
- If you are using a projector, carry a spare bulb.
- Rehearse the visual aids.
- Switch off the projector between slides.

- Use a pointer not a finger to draw attention.
- Line up the slides before switching the projector on.

Whatever you use, remember visual aids are there to *clarify,* not to add to the *confusion.* Make sure:

- The purpose of the visual aid is clear.
- The visual aid is really necessary.
- The visual aid is memorable.
- The visual aid is legible.
- The visual aid will convey the meaning you intend.
- The visual aid will be understood.

## Dealing with the audience

The audience is a key part of your presentation, so you must get the most out of them. That involves understanding what makes them tick, what they are thinking and how they learn.

### How humans retain facts

The human animal communicates through the five senses as follows:

- Sight - 75 per cent
- Hearing - 13 per cent
- Touch, taste and smell - 12 per cent.

Individuals will recall 10 per cent of what they hear after three days; 20 per cent of what they see after three days; 65 per cent of what they see and hear after three days. Thus to extend retention, use visual effects.

### Self conditioning

People are conditioned to the world about them. They relate all that is said to their own experiences. To enable them to understand more fully the import of presentations give them 'induced conditioning', ie set them a picture of a world to relate to.

### Generalised terms

Avoid the use of generalised terms such as:

- some
- average
- moderate
- several

which all mean different things to different people. Use the word and they will start to think about its meaning rather than about what you are saying.

### Statements

Three types of statement are used in communication:

- *Factual* - in which a fact is stated.
- *Value judgements* - in which you express your opinion and make it clear that it is your opinion. Don't make value judgements sound like facts.
- *Inferential* - in which the interpretation of the statement is left to the listener.

Don't use the inferential statement if you want to keep audience attention. They will only start to think about their own opinions and fail to listen to you.

## Body language

Understanding body language is the art of seeing what others are thinking. It is invaluable if you are making a presentation; or even any kind of communication.

### The obvious

Keep an eye out for the obvious indicators that things are not going too well:

- looking at the watch;
- shaking the wrist to see if the watch is still going;
- pretend yawns;
- sneak looks at the clock or a neighbour's watch;
- touching the watch while still maintaining eye contact.

Quite obviously, they all mean 'This has gone on long enough.'

### The less obvious

All body language is obvious when you think about it; most people don't think about it and so miss the feedback available from the audience at all times. Watch for some of the following:

| | |
|---|---|
| *Boredom* | Head in hands, chin resting on palms, body slumped in seat |

| | |
|---|---|
| *Anxiety* | Wringing hands together |
| *Defensive, unco-operative* | Arms crossed, ankles crossed, sitting well back in seat |
| *Apprehension* | Hands on knees, possibly holding on to material of trousers, ankles crossed |
| *Attentive, but not convinced* | Slumped in seat, legs stretched out, one hand hanging by side, the other resting on the knee |
| *Needs clarification* | Sitting upright, one leg crossed over the other thigh at right angles with opposite hand holding ankle |
| *Open, willing participant* | Sitting well back in seat, legs apart, arms resting on knees, hand in open gesture |
| *Confident superiority* | Laid back in chair, hands clasped behind head |
| *Confident* | Finger tips together to form a pyramid shape with the hands, sitting well back in chair |
| *Reserved, confident* | Sitting back, fingers interlinked |
| *Interested* | Leaning forward in seat |

Obviously, the closer you get to an individual, the more you can see of his or her gestures, and the more body language you can read. Talking to a group, even a small group, will not let you get near enough to read anything but the broadest facial and hand gesures. They are:

| | |
|---|---|
| *Negative evaluation* | Resting chin on thumb, index finger under the nose, or fingers to ear lobe, or fingers to corner of the eye |
| *Exasperation* | Hand to the back of neck at hairline with facial grimace |
| *Wanting to interrupt* | Fingers to open mouth (not a yawn) |
| *Dissatisfied* | Resting side of face on the palm of one hand |
| *Defensive* | Head down, no eye contact |
| *Open* | Head up, total eye contact |
| *Interested* | Head on one side, total eye contact |

## Timetable checklists

When you are preparing for a presentation always have your presentation notebook handy.

*Two days prior to presentation*

1. List attendees

2. Prepare name badges

3. Assemble handouts and any demonstration material

*One day prior to presentaton*

1. Full rehearsal

2. Set up all facilities (if possible)

3. Check equipment

4. Check direction signs to presentation room

5. Confirm refreshment arrangements

6. Reconfirm any other speakers

7. Set up contingency plan

*Presentation day*

1. Arrive at least one hour early

2. Review agenda

3. Check refreshments

4. Check facilities and equipment

5. Set up reception

6. Check direction signs

7. Register audience

## Equipment checklist

- ☐ Lectern
- ☐ Speaker's console
- ☐ Black/whiteboard
- ☐ Flipchart
- ☐ Microphones
- ☐ Overhead projector
- ☐ 16-mm projector
- ☐ Slide projector
- ☐ Screen(s)
- ☐ TV
- ☐ Video
- ☐ Extension leads
- ☐ Power points
- ☐ Agendas
- ☐ Seating plans
- ☐ Handouts
- ☐ Brochures

- ☐ Pens
- ☐ Flipchart paper
- ☐ Flipchart markers
- ☐ Overhead projector pointer
- ☐ Spare acetates or roll
- ☐ Acetate pens
- ☐ Adhesive tape
- ☐ Paper
- ☐ Scissors
- ☐ Badges
- ☐ Name badges
- ☐ OHP slides
- ☐ Videos
- ☐ Films
- ☐ 35-mm slides

# Further Reading from Kogan Page

*The Action-Centred Leader,* John Adair, 1988
*Don't Do. Delegate! The Secret Power of Successful Managers,* James M Jenks and John M Kelly, 1986
*Effective Interviewing,* John Fletcher, 1988
*Essential Facts for Managers,* British Institute of Management, 1988
*Essential Management Checklists,* Jeffrey P Davidson, 1987
*The First-Time Manager,* M J Morris
*A Handbook of Management Techniques,* Michael Armstrong, 1986
*How to Be an Even Better Manager,* Michael Armstrong, 1988
*How to Make Meetings Work,* Malcolm Peel, 1988
*Never Take No For An Answer,* Samfrits Le Poole, 1987
*The Practice of Successful Business Management* Kenneth Winckles, 1986
*Profits from Improved Productivity,* Fiona Halse and John Humphrey, 1988
*Readymade Business Letters,* Jim Dening, 1986
*Readymade Business Speeches,* Barry Turner, 1989
*Readymade Interview Questions,* Malcolm Peel, 1988
*So You Think Your Business Needs a Computer,* Khalid Aziz, 1986
*Winning Strategies for Managing People: A Task Directed Guide,* Robert Irwin and Rita Wolenik, 1986

**Better Management Skills series**

*Effective Meeting Skills*
*Effective Performance Appraisals*
*Effective Presentation Skills*
*The Fifty-Minute Supervisor*
*How to Communicate Effectively*
*How to Develop a Positive Attitude*
*How to Motivate People*
*Make Every Minute Count*
*Successful Negotiation*
*Team Building*